PARISH ANNIVERSAI

In Celebration of our parish anniversary we will have a parish retreat beginning with weekend Masses March 23/24. The retreat will continue on the evenings of March 24, 25, and 26 with liturgies at 7 pm. During the day there will be opportunities for individual sessions with the retreat director, Father Ed Wills.

Father Ed is not your typical priest. He has been a US Naval officer, a corporate executive, a small business entrepreneur, and a working musician. But, God's call has always been close to his heart.

Raised in the Southern Evangelical tradition, Fr. Ed was licensed to preach by the Grace Gospel Fellowship when he was only 18. He developed an interest in historic Christianity while a student at Oral Roberts University. One of his Greek professors challenged him, "If you want to understand the writings of the apostles, you need to read the writings of their students." This challenge led him to study the earliest Church Fathers. What he discovered was that the Catholic Church maintained a consistent tradition of faith and authority from the apostles to the present day. He did his graduate studies in Theology at the University of Dallas, a Catholic University. After serving as a Bible Church pastor, Ed was ordained in the Charismatic Episcopal Church and finally committed to the Roman Catholic Church in 2000. He was ordained a Catholic priest in 2018 at the age of 64 and is currently serving as pastor of Our Lady of Hope Catholic Community.

Father Ed is the author of two books, "Where Do I Go from Here?" and "Learning to Listen to God". He has been married for 38 years and has three daughters and three grandchildren.

Needless to say, Father Ed brings a unique perspective to St. Ann's anniversary retreat. How does God's love and grace guide us in the practical world of everyday life? Did Jesus really mean it when he promised "life to the full?" Come with an open heart to discover new depth to your faith.

Where Do I Go From Here?

A Guidebook for Life's Transitions

by
Ed Wills

Acknowledgments

Books do not arise out of thin air, but are the result of years of hard work and the collaboration of many. This book was years in the making, but arises from a lifetime of study and experiences. There are many I would like to thank for their contribution to this work. I apologize for all I inadvertently left out.

I extend my deepest gratitude to Napoleon Hill, Dale Carnegie, Norman Vincent Peale, Zig Ziglar, James Rohn, Jack Canfield, Lou Tice, Tony Evans, Deepak Chopra, Eckhart Tolle, and countless others who laid the foundation I attempted to build upon in this work. Of the preceding list, I only personally met Zig Ziglar, but all have been my mentors. Occasionally, I quoted directly from some of them. I want the reader to be aware that all contributed profoundly to the concepts I present in this work.

I want to thank Heather Beers for taking on the monumental task of editing this work for me. I honestly don't think this book would be worth reading without her help.

Father Samuel Anthony Morello, OCD first taught me the principles of breath, focus, and guided meditation. Dr. Ladd Carlston of Mind in Motion greatly expanded my understanding of relaxation and energy. These and other mentors helped me with those principles from which I developed the concept of *Stillness* presented here.

I am grateful to Denise Mills of LeaderFuel NOW, who was a help with many of the concepts presented here. But I am especially grateful for her friendship, support, and encouragement.

Finally, I want to thank my wife, Cheryl, who is my number one cheerleader, and our three lovely daughters who are a never-ending source of inspiration to me. Cheryl faithfully read each manuscript as this book evolved into the work you have today. She continuously moved me to make each concept simpler and clearer. All readers should be grateful to her. Also, a special thanks to our daughter Annie who worked tirelessly on the musical background of the guided meditation audios.

DEDICATION:
To my family,
who have endured my many
philosophical and vocational searchings
from which this book emerged.

Table of Contents

viii

Introduction

The mind is its own place,
  and in itself
  can make a heaven of Hell,
  a hell of Heaven.
-John Milton

My Personal Story

All of life is a transition. The sun rises, crosses the sky, then sets. A child is born, discovers the world, marries, and then passes life on to the next generation. A worker receives training and education, chooses a career, changes his or her career, and then retires. An idea blossoms, becomes a book, is rewritten into a different book, and then finds a reader.

I first wrote this book as a guide for first-time entrepreneurs to encourage them as they undertook their terrifying journey into small business ownership. After all, I had been successful in several business endeavors. In fact, the original title for the book was "How to Succeed at Whatever You Do."

With the crash of 2008, my businesses struggled, and I wondered if I was truly qualified to offer guidance to others. I set the book down and turned my attention inward, trying to rediscover my own confidence in troubling times. I found myself revisiting the principles outlined in this book repeatedly, each time with increased fervor.

My breakthrough came when I implemented a form of meditation I call *Stillness*, which became the catalyst for giving these principles explosive intensity in my own life. I had meditated for decades for relaxation and my own spirituality, but I had not applied meditation techniques to the success process. Through the practice of *Stillness*, I found insights and intuitions I had not imagined possible.

One of my most powerful realizations is that success is not something you "do." Success is who you "are." *You* are the measurement of your success, not your bank account. That's why many highly successful people have suffered tremendous setbacks, even multiple bankruptcies, and still make their way back to the top. Once you find and empower the success inside you, everything else associated with success will fall into place.

It is helpful at this point to think of this book as a roadmap for a journey. Focus less on the information and concepts you learn here and more on your personal passage. You may want to keep a notebook handy in which you can enter thoughts or ideas as you think of them. Allow any portion to serve as a springboard into your own thoughts. It is my sincere hope and prayer that you will find the ideas, principles, and practices presented in this book helpful to you in your own transition from wherever you are to wherever you want to go.

The Practice of *Stillness*

Finding some quiet time in your life, I think, is hugely important.
- Mariel Hemmingway

Every day I practice *Stillness*. I sit in a comfortable chair, relax, and focus on my breathing. I pay attention to the sensations of my body. I feel the air pass in through my nostrils. I sense its coolness. I notice aromas being carried in the air around me. I feel the weight of my body. I sense the resistance of the chair supporting me. I hear ambient sounds. Soft music in the background. The monotonous drone of traffic somewhere in the distance. I empty my mind. The endless internal chatter that drives us all to madness ceases. I am still. I am whole.

I may just relax, breathe, and focus on the *Stillness*. I may go through a guided meditation, providing a planned input into my subconscious. I may just allow my mind to flow freely. I allow my creative imagination to take over and go wherever it likes, without judgment. Often in those times, I experience some of my greatest inspirations.

You may wonder what is the difference between surrendering to your creative imagination (what I call *Stillness*) and daydreaming. Daydreaming is the mental pursuit of some fantasy or aspiration. *Stillness* is the emptying of your mind of personal pursuits and allowing your intuitive inner self to lead you into places that can bring insight and healing.

It has been my experience that people know the answer to their most pressing problems, both business and personal. However, our conscious minds tend to fill with constant chatter that's often negative and destructive. The practice of *Stillness* enables you to silence the internal accuser and listen to the quiet inner voice of solace. Some refer to this as intuition. To others, it is the voice of God. Whatever label you give it, it is free and available to all who embrace truth in the innermost reaches of their heart and mind.

Inspiration comes to different people in different ways. Some write. Others get great ideas in the shower. Albert Einstein played the violin when working on a particularly vexing problem. Warren Buffett's idea of becoming a principal investor in Bank of America came while taking a bath.[1]

Many great business leaders turn to hobbies for distraction when they are faced with their most serious challenges. Golf is a standard among CEO's around the world. A global concierge service called Quintessentially assists numerous CEO's with their hobbies. CEO distractions include Formula 1 racecar driving, paleontology, archeology, and combat training. The great thinkers of the ages consistently tell us that often the only way to solve a problem is to stop thinking about it.

Our creative imaginations are always at work, examining issues, developing solutions, and investigating new directions. However, we are too busy with our daily lives and business to notice. The practice of *Stillness* allows us to listen to our creative imaginations and learn from them. Our creative imaginations are connected to our subconscious minds in a subliminal intersection that lies just below our surface thinking. Our subconscious minds are able to process much more information than our conscious minds. We should pay attention to them. That doesn't mean that we need to take every idea that we have when we are meditating and run with it as if it was sent to us directly from God.

In the Bible, there is a story about a prophet who heard God in a still, small voice. I have found that voice to be an excellent guide. The daily practice of *Stillness* will help you learn to find the still, small voice within you. I caution everyone not to confuse his or her inner voice with an infallible divine oracle. The intuitive inner voice of your subconscious is not infallible. However, it is a much better processor than your conscious mind.

The first step in intentionally connecting with your intuitive inner self is learning to breathe.

Intentional Breathing

The Lord gives breath to the people of the earth, and His Spirit to those who walk upon it.
- Isaiah the Prophet

Intentional breathing is an integral part of many of life's endeavors, especially those that are "on the edge." Navy Seals train in intentional breathing techniques that enable them to stay calm and keep their wits about them in situations so intensely dangerous that most of us would run from them without thinking. High performance jet pilots like those in the Navy's Blue Angels or the Air Force's Thunderbirds practice intentional breathing to keep a steady rhythm while experiencing velocity induced gravitational forces so intense that they would render the average person unconscious.

The practice of *Stillness* also uses intentional breathing techniques. *Stillness* is not dangerous like fighting terrorists or flying high performance jets. However, the use of intentional breathing can bring intensity to the experience that will maximize the physical, mental, and spiritual benefits of the meditation.

For the guided meditations practiced in this book you will need to know five types of breathing: the Cleansing Breath, the Upper Breath (sometimes called "Heart Breathing"), the Lower Breath (sometimes called "Abdominal Breathing"), Balanced Breathing, and the Salutogenic Breath.

As you might guess, the Upper Breath focuses on filling your upper lungs with air. You should feel your chest expand. Your shoulders should visibly rise. Your mental point of focus should be your heart.

The Lower Breath focuses on filling your lower lungs with air. You should feel your lungs filling like a barrel, from the bottom up. Your stomach should visibly rise. Your mental point of focus should be your abdomen. Don't be confused and think you shouldn't allow air into your lower lungs if your are practicing Upper Breathing, or don't try to prevent air from entering your upper lungs if you're practicing Lower Breathing. The issue is focus. Where you focus your breath-energy is far more important than where the air actually goes.

Before we practice breathing, look at the following chart. Go ahead and fill out the "Before Exercise" column. We will fill out the rest later, after you have practiced the breathing exercises.

DISCOVERING THE POWER OF BREATH

Rate how you are currently feeling in the following areas of your life on a scale of 1—10.

First, be sure to record how you are feeling in all the above areas before you begin the exercise.

Second, take 5—10 upper breaths following the directions in this chapter. Now, rate yourself in each area again using the same 1—10 scale.

ATTITUDE	Before Exercise	After Upper Breaths	After Lower Breaths
Self Confidence			
Energy			
Creativity			
Imagination			
Sensory Awareness			
Peacefulness			
Self Control			

Finally, take 5—10 lower breaths following the directions in this chapter. Now, rate yourself in each area again using the same 1—10 scale.

Did you notice any improvements in your energy, self-confidence, creativity, imagination or sensory awareness after taking time to focus on your breath?

Printable worksheets can be downloaded from
WhereDoIGoFromHere.net

The Upper Breath

Sit in a relaxed, comfortable position. Breathe naturally, through your nose if possible. Your eyes can be open or closed, whichever feels more comfortable. Think about your heart. Imagine your heart pumping life throughout your body. Take your fingertips and place them on your chest near your heart. Now sit up as straight as possible. Take a rapid deep breath focusing on filling your chest with as much air as you possibly can. You should feel your fingertips rise. Hold for about one second, and then exhale through your mouth. Repeat this 5-10 times, each time imagining breathing life and light into your heart. When you have finished, relax and breathe normally again, through your nose if possible.

Consider how you feel now. Has your energy level changed? How is your self-confidence? Are you more aware of sounds and smells in the room? Do you feel more creative or imaginative than you did a few moments before? Take a minute to record your feelings using a 1-10 scale in the preceding chart.

The Lower Breath

Sit in a relaxed, comfortable position. Breathe naturally, through your nose if possible. Think about the depth of your soul, your innermost being. Imagine your deepest hopes and longings. Imagine a "you" that's not filled with stress and concerns, but with power and possibilities. Take your hands and place them on your abdomen, just below your navel. Now sit up as straight as possible. Take a rapid deep breath focusing on filling your lower lungs with as much air as you possibly can. You should feel your stomach rise. Hold for about one second, and then exhale through your mouth. Repeat this 5-10 times, each time imagining breathing life and light into your soul. When you have finished, relax and breathe normally again, through your nose if possible.

Consider how you feel now. Has your energy level changed? How is your self-confidence? Are you more aware of sounds and smells in the room? Do you feel more peaceful or calm than you did a few moments before? Take a minute to record your feelings using a 1-10 scale in the preceding chart.

If you're like most people, you will have noticed a significant elevation of your feelings of confidence, creative imagination, and perhaps even joy. At the physiological level, you have pumped extra oxygen into the frontal cortex of your brain by coupling deep breathing with imaginative focus. The frontal cortex controls the mental processes of imagination, creativity, confidence, joy, and spirituality. If you did not notice any difference, don't be concerned. It will come with practice.

Now that you know the upper and lower breath exercise, take 2 minutes any time you feel the need to increase your confidence or creativity.

Balanced Breath

Balanced Breathing is a slow rhythmic breathing in which the inhale and the exhale are the same approximate duration. In Balanced Breathing, a four-second inhale is followed by a four-second exhale. A six-second inhale is followed by a six-second exhale and so forth. In Balanced Breathing, you're not focusing on a particular part of the body as in heart or abdominal breathing. Instead, you may focus on the breath itself, the coolness of the air passing through your nostrils, the rise and fall of your chest, or even on simply counting "In - 2 - 3 - 4. Out - 2- 3 - 4."

Balanced Breathing will be the majority of the breathing practiced during the guided meditations in this book. During our meditations here, you will be instructed what to focus on during the Balanced Breathing. For example, you will be directed, "Breathe in peace. Breathe out stress." You will also be given mental visuals to focus on.

In Balanced Breathing, you may breathe in and out through your nose. Or, if you prefer, you may breathe in through your nose and out through your mouth. When exhaling through the mouth, it is best to purse your lips slightly to form a backpressure, optimizing oxygen absorption in the lungs. However, if you have sinus issues and nasal breathing is difficult or distracting, it is okay to inhale through your mouth.

Balanced Breathing should be simple and normal. Little thought is required. Once a pattern is established, just continue breathing naturally, allowing your mind to focus on the guided meditation.

Cleansing Breath

The purpose of the Cleansing Breath is to expel stale air from your lungs. It can be done at any time during the day to refresh your lungs and help them maximize oxygen utilization. It is a great exercise to use before beginning the practice of *Stillness*.

Relax and inhale through your nose. Fill your lungs as much as possible. Hold for one second. Now exhale forcefully contracting your diaphragm and pushing up with your stomach muscles until all the air is expelled from your lungs. Repeat these two or three times. If you start to feel dizzy, just relax and breathe normally for a while. It will pass quickly.

Salutogenic Breath

Salutogenesis literally means "The beginning of healing." In meditation breathing Salutogenic Breath occurs naturally, unaided, and unexpectedly. However, you will know when it happens. It appears like an extra breath. A Salutogenic Breath may occur at the beginning of a breath. You will simply notice that a particular breath is much longer and deeper than you planned. Or, it may occur at the end of a breath. You will complete your anticipated inhale, and then you will suddenly draw in an extra breath. A little more oxygen will be infused into your system.

If you yawn during your meditation, it is a good thing. A yawn is a form of Salutogenic Breath. You draw in extra oxygen. Your muscles naturally tense, and then relax.

With eight Olympic medals, speed skater Apolo Anton Ohno is the most decorated American Winter Olympic athlete of all time. If you include his World Championship races, Ohno has won a total of 14 gold medals, 10 silver medals, and 11 bronze medals. He surprised millions of television viewing sports fans when he produced a big yawn before his race in the 2010 Vancouver Games. He later explained that he did it on purpose. "It makes me feel better," he said. "It gets the oxygen in and the nerves out." [2]

Enjoy your yawn.

BOOK ONE

DISCOVER YOUR PATH

CHAPTER 1

Do Your Core Values, Talents, and Passions Really Matter?

Keep your faith in something Greater than you, and keep doing what you love. When you do what you love, you will find the way to get it out to the world.
- Judy Collins

Why is deciding what you want one of the hardest decisions to make in life? There are many reasons for indecision:

- You're afraid of what you might miss if you choose one option over another.
- You are trying to make a decision that will please others.
- All choices involve an element of the unknown, and that scares you.
- You're still collecting information and analyzing your choices.

All of the preceding reasons have one thing in common – fear. People are afraid of missing out, afraid of being embarrassed, or afraid of making a mistake.

Fear never serves your best interest. It is wise to be cautious when working with poisonous snakes, but being afraid will only cause you to make a mistake that might lead to an unwanted snakebite. Some would say, "'Shouldn't we be afraid of God?' Didn't Solomon write, 'The fear of the Lord is the beginning of wisdom.'?" The translation is unfortunate and has caused generations to see

God as someone to fear. It has always been difficult to reconcile that concept of God with the teachings of Jesus who taught his disciples to call God, "Daddy." The Hebrew word for fear would better be translated 'awesome presence' or 'complete devotion'. It is the emotion that can truly cause one to tremble. The Quakers were so named because of the trembling they would experience during public prayer. The trembling was not from fear, though, but from the depth of devotion being in God's awesome presence. In the Old Testament, the *fear* of the Lord is said to bring joy and delight. That's far from our concept of fear.

Perhaps you tell me that you have no problem at all deciding what you want. You know exactly what you want. Of course, what you want today is different from what you wanted last week, which was different from what you wanted last month, which was different from what you wanted last year. If that's you, then your issue is not making a decision, but making decisions too quickly without thorough thought and commitment. Your decisions are not really decisions at all. You're just sampling.

What is your behavior in a restaurant?

- You go to a restaurant and stare at the menu. You change your mind four times, and then when the waiter arrives, you order something completely different.
- You always visit the newest restaurant and look for something you have never tried before. Each new restaurant and each new dish is an adventure.
- You go to the same restaurant each week. You don't even bother to open the menu and order the same thing you ordered in that restaurant the last six times you were there.

Different people demonstrate the same behavior for different reasons. Having a hard time making up your mind about your lunch doesn't necessarily mean you're a weak decision maker, but it might. Eating the same thing all the time doesn't necessarily mean you're in a rut. Perhaps you know from experience that there is only one thing on the menu you like.

Let me make everyone comfortable. None of the preceding behaviors is wrong. They are just expressions of someone's personality. Our personalities engender behaviors that can be construed as positive or negative, but the behaviors themselves are neither positive nor negative. The same behavior may be positive or negative depending on the circumstance. For example, do you consider slicing your neighbor open with a knife to be a negative behavior? Most people do. However, if you're a surgeon performing an appendectomy, it is a very positive behavior. What makes the difference is the motive or goal of the act. While a certain behavior is not in itself positive or negative, it may or may not support your personal goals or purpose in life. What I hope to accomplish in this book is to give you some tools to choose what behaviors will be supportive for you, behaviors that will move you toward your goals.

Let's back up. Before we can have goals, we must first understand our values.

Jason was a professional salesman. He enjoyed considerable financial success but felt disconnected with himself. After more than 10 years as a sales professional, he discovered there was no relationship between his personal values and his business goals. Like many, he sought success through endless training, motivation, and hard work. Like many sales people, he traveled a great deal while building a family. Crisis brewed as cracks developed in the foundation of his family. Relationships strained, but Jason didn't realize what was going on until he and his wife went shopping for new furniture. To his shock, he realized he was trying to decorate his house to look like a hotel room. That's when he decided that his world was upside down. He took a weekend to do some serious soul searching and discover his true values. "That weekend," says Jason, "changed everything." Once he knew his core values, he was able to reshape his life in a way that supported his values of relationship and family. Jason took a job closer to home with fewer travel days and participated actively in nurturing his children. "I will never go back to what I was," reflects Jason. "I only wish I had discovered this principle sooner."

Many people make goals or resolutions, work at them for a few weeks, and then drop them. Some very disciplined people may work on their goals for years and accomplish all of them, only to find they are unhappy and unfulfilled. The problem in both of these scenarios is the same: They drafted goals that conflicted with their core values. A lot of books and CD's in the marketplace talk about goal setting. However, unless you align your goals with your true core values, they will not work for you. In fact, your goals can work against you, making you miserable instead of happy. For example, if one of your true values is solitude, setting a career goal in sales just might leave you despondent.

What we want are goals that make us happy. Achieving a goal, any goal, takes a good deal of effort. If the goal makes you happy, the time and energy you spend reaching it is much easier. And that's why core values, talents, and passions really do matter.

What Are Your True Core Values?

If we are to go forward, we must go back and rediscover those precious values - that all reality hinges on moral foundations and that all reality has spiritual control.
- Martin Luther King, Jr.

Our core values shape the way we perceive the world and make our decisions. Yet, many people never consider them. Our core values work like our immune system. When we are healthy, we tend not to think about it. When we engage in behavior that damages our immune system - like not getting the right nutrients or missing sleep - it breaks down, and we get sick. Too often, we take medications that remove some of the symptoms of being sick. We would do better to strengthen our immune system so we can be truly healthy again. In the same way, our core values work to keep us happy. When we live our lives in such a way that conflicts with our core values, we become dissatisfied and restless. We might cover up our dissatisfaction with distractions like entertainment, hobbies, or fantasies. We would do better to rearrange our lives in such a way that our daily activities support our core values instead of conflict with them. First, we must identify exactly what our core values are.

Typically, our core values lie beneath the surface. We are only aware of them in times of great stress or great joy. The following exercise will help you identify your true core values.

Core Values Exercise

List Five Special Times or Events

Think of times in your life when you were the happiest.
Where were you? What were you doing? What made that
time so enjoyable or even magical? Were you alone? Were
you with others? How did they add or detract from the
experience? What were your feelings? Did you want the
time to last forever? Is there anything you can do now to
make that feeling come back?

In the following exercise, list five times or experiences that
were especially meaningful to you. Only list times or
experiences that were very special to you. Do not
superimpose someone else's values on your memories.
Perhaps the birth of your first child was a very special
moment to you. On the other hand, maybe you were just
exhausted and glad it was over. There is no right or wrong
here, and no one is going to read it but you, so be
completely honest.

Why Were Those Experiences Important?

Next, go back and read each experience carefully. Ask
yourself, "What made those experiences so important to
me?" "Why did they have such an impact?" Look for
common threads. What do all these experiences have in
common? What made those special times so special? Write
the reasons why those experiences made you happy.

List Your Core Values

Finally, read over the reasons your special times were
special. What values are repeatedly revealed? What values
stand out? For example, if all of your special times involve

being with your family then what made those times special might be sharing moments with people you love. A core value would likely be *Family*. Perhaps your special times were catching your first fish, winning an athletic event, graduating from college, and getting a big promotion. The reasons those times were special might be that you fulfilled your goals and were recognized by people you respect. Your core value might be *Pride of Accomplishment*.

Here are some possible core values:
Creativity
Integrity
Pride of Accomplishment
Perseverance
Family
Spirituality
Community
Recognition
Philanthropy
Generosity

Five Events That Were Special To You

1. _____

2. _____

3. _____

4. _____

5. _____

Reasons Those Special Times Were Special

1. _____

2. _____

3. _____

4. _____

5. _____

Your Core Values

1. _____

2. _____

3. _____

4. _____

5. _____

Talent Reflection

*An artist is not a special kind of man; rather, every man is
a special kind of artist.*
-Meister Eckhart

Sam Finley was the epitome of a starving artist. His work
was actually quite good, but his shyness and lack of self-
esteem kept him from showing his art to anyone. Still, he
was an artist through and through. He couldn't keep himself
from painting. He had no job but existed on a subsistence
income in the form of a monthly disability check. He spent
his time rummaging through trash piles and dumpsters for
scraps of wood, a discarded door, a piece of Masonite,
anything on which he could paint. He hid all his paintings
in a basement storage unit of an old automotive shop
converted to small offices. My daughter, my wife, and I
opened a small coffee shop in the building and met Sam.
After awhile we eased into his tight inner circle and were
allowed to see the paintings in the storage unit. We were
astounded. We had already begun having regular art
displays in our coffee shop and insisted he show his pieces.
He slowly relented and told us we could show his work.
We put him on the schedule. The day before his first art
show, he reversed himself and refused. We would have
none of it and just brought his pieces out of the basement
ourselves. He continued to protest but there was nothing he
could do. We displayed his work for a month. Local
customers purchased several of Sam's pieces. As it
happened, our local congressional representative held a
town meeting in our shop, which was a central gathering
place for our small town. He loved Sam's work and
purchased a piece. From then on, the congressman spoke
often about the amazing artist he discovered among his
constituents. What followed were gallery showings, one-
man shows, and corporate commissions. Sam now paints

on real canvas, and his paintings command several thousand dollars each.

You've got talent. You may not be a musician or artist, but you still have underlying talents that can move you naturally and easily to success. In fact, being overtly talented in an area such as music or art can often mask important underlying talents that are less obvious. Your underlying talents help you determine what kind of career you will most likely be good at, or what type of role in an organization would suit you best.

To illustrate the point, how many former professional athletes can you think of who, upon retiring from professional sports, took up careers as public accountants? There may be some out there, but I can't think of any. That's because a key underlying talent for a professional-quality athlete is the drive to make things happen. Make the tackle. Score the goal. Hit the home run. A key underlying talent for a public accountant is the drive to analyze and accurately record what has already happened. The former athlete is more likely to seek an entrepreneurial career after sports, where he or she can continue to "make things happen."

Underlying Talent Exercise

Look over the following chart. Rate the statements on a scale of 1-3 as follows:

    1 - This is just like me. I almost always feel this way.
    2 - Sometimes I feel this way, sometimes not.
    3 - I almost never feel this way.

Statement	Rank	Trait
Life is a competition. I always need to end up on top.		Competitor
I hate planning. I usually just get started and work out the details later.		Doer
I don't plan too far ahead. I like to do whatever strikes me at the moment.		Spontaneous
One plan is not enough for me. I always have multiple plans and backup plans.		Strategist
The only way to make sure a job is done right is to do it myself.		Soloist
I always find the best person for the job, and then monitor them closely.		Coordinator
I am most comfortable when someone gives me clear instructions and goals.		Employee
Life is a game. Whoever dies with the most toys wins.		Materialist
Family and friends come first. Job and personal satisfaction come after.		Relationship

The most important things in life are enjoying inner peace and doing good in the world.		Spiritual
I tell people how it is, and they shape up or ship out.		Commander
I give people the tools to help them discover their own purpose.		Facilitator
I enjoy passing information through creative stories and illustrations.		Communicator
I feel other's joys and pains.		Empathizer
I won't stop arguing until everyone admits I'm right.		Antagonist
Careful planning and implementation is the key to success.		Builder
Once I set myself on a goal, nothing can get in my way.		Bulldog
I want to make sure everyone is working together happily.		Peacemaker
I see my future clearly and know I can get there.		Visionary
I love to gather information before making a decision.		Learner
I love to gather information just so I can know more.		Intellectual
Whatever happens, I will succeed.		Optimist

Now go back and circle the traits associated with all those ranked number one. They indicate some of your underlying talents. You probably have others. These will suffice to give you a starting place as you plan career or life goals.

If your number ones included commander and bulldog, you might want to consider a career in the military or in another rigid organization where your forceful leadership style will be rewarded.

If you ranked high as an intellectual, a learner, and a communicator, a career as an educator or in an organization where the dissemination of information is an important aspect of the job can be rewarding.

Many of us think that other's talents are better or more important than ours are. The academic may inwardly wish he or she were an athlete. The athlete may wish he or she were a rocket scientist. A key to success is to forget the "if only's" and focus on the skills and talents that come naturally to you.

Where Is Your Passion?

Always go with your passions. Never ask yourself if it's realistic or not.
- Deepak Chopra

Has anyone ever made a lot of money doing what he or she hates? Sure. It's actually quite common. But has anyone ever been truly successful doing what they hate? Only if their definition of success doesn't include personal happiness and fulfillment. We live in a society with many options. We can choose to go to college or vocational school. We can choose to be an entrepreneur or an employee. We can choose to work for a venture capitalist or a non-profit. Whatever your choice, your level of success will greatly depend on choosing options that support your core values and that allow you to do things you're truly passionate about. That's because doing a job well requires a great deal of time, effort, and personal commitment. Devoting yourself to something for which you have no passion is very difficult and unrewarding.

It's alluring to go after a job in an industry that you heard was easy or profitable. You can certainly be successful at it, if what you want is a 9-5 job, being home evenings and weekends, reaching middle management, and retiring on social security plus a modest 401k. There is nothing wrong with that model. Just be sure that's truly what you want from life.

Many people work at whatever job they can get and then seek personal fulfillment from relationships and hobbies. The risk is that relationships can change, and someday you may not always be able to perform your hobbies. There often comes a time when people begin to feel empty and search for meaning in what they do. That may be why you're reading this book.

Naval Ravikant is a computer genius. He received degrees in computer science and economics from Dartmouth College. Soon after his arrival in Silicon Valley, Ravikant became known as an Internet guru. However, writing computer code was not his passion. Even though he was a technical expert, his passion was the people side of the Internet business. What he truly enjoyed was connecting investors and entrepreneurs. He then became one of the founders of Angel List, an Internet based service that enables entrepreneurs to pitch their ideas and plans to potential investors. Entrepreneurs like the service because it streamlines their search for investors. Investors like it because of Naval's experience in determining which ideas have merit and which entrepreneurs have what it takes to make it happen. Naval Ravikant has now helped more than 300 entrepreneurs find the funding necessary to put their ideas into action.[3]

Find Your Passion Exercise

Ask yourself these questions.

If I could start all over again, what would I change?

My Education

My Career

My Location

What activities make me truly happy?

What is it about those activities that makes me happy? (For example: the people I am with, the competition, the sense of accomplishment, inner peace.)

28

If all jobs paid the same, what would I do for a living?

If I'm not doing that right now, WHY NOT?

What is True Success?

*Always be yourself, express yourself, have faith in yourself,
do not go out and look for a successful personality and
duplicate it.*
- Bruce Lee

I use the word 'success' throughout this book. However, the
term is often vague and can be misleading. That's because it
holds profoundly different meanings for different people.
One person's success is another's hell on earth. The
definition of 'success' I use throughout this book is *finding
satisfaction and fulfillment in an endeavor you're truly
passionate about.* Ultimately, you must define success for
yourself. It will be different from others' definitions, and
you should be okay with that. One way to make yourself
truly miserable is to try to fulfill someone else's definition
of success.

Mr. Clark was the school custodian where I attended
elementary school. He found great joy in keeping our
school spotlessly clean. He could always be found in the
hallways, with dust mop in hand, humming a little tune. He
would smile and offer bits of Southern wisdom to the
children who passed by. "Study hard. Make something of
yourself. But don't forget to do good, because in the end all

you have is your good name." Most of us don't consider school custodian to be a highly successful career, but he was truly successful. He found joy and fulfillment in his life and work. His father was likely a slave. In the South before the civil rights movement, he may have never considered a higher paying career. But I never saw him without a smile on his face, and I benefit from his legacy to this day.

Don't think I'm saying you have to be poor to be happy. I just want to be clear that money is not the sole measure of success. However, money is important, even essential, to most of us.

Do What You Love
(and Make Money While You're at It)

The exciting part of knowing your values, talents, and passions is that you can envision a way to make money through their commercial application. Perhaps family is one of your core values. You might look for jobs close to home or start a business that you could operate from your home, where you will not only be close to your family, but you will also be able to involve them in some aspects of your business. If your values include spirituality, working in a health-related field could incorporate a spiritual dimension. If recognition or philanthropy is included in your list, a business that incorporates community involvement might be just the ticket.

David Filo loved computers. He received a BS in Computer Engineering from Tulane University followed by an MS from Stanford. He was intrigued by the Internet and, with his friend Jerry Yang, created a directory of websites called, "Jerry and Dave's Guide to the World Wide Web."

The directory was renamed "Yahoo!" and became an early Internet sensation.[4]

Michael Dell also loved computers. He bought his first calculator when he was seven years old. When he got his first computer, an Apple II, he took it apart to understand the hardware of computing. Unlike Filo, Dell did not pursue an education in computing, but majored in pre-med, planning to be a doctor. However, he could not keep himself away from computers and earned money in college upgrading and repairing other students' computers. At age 27, he became the youngest CEO to have his enterprise, Dell Computers, named a Fortune 500 Company.

Following your passion doesn't always lead to great financial rewards. Sarah quit her job, cashed in her retirement, and moved to Africa to teach literacy to children. Financial wealth is not one of her objectives, but her life has never been richer.

Angela's passion was the American Soap Opera. When she and her husband returned from a vacation, she was uncertain about the current plots in her favorite soaps. She had no idea what had happened while she was gone. She wondered if people would pay money to be kept up to date on the soap operas they missed. Soap Opera Digest was born. Within 10 years, the magazine had over a million subscribers.

Whatever your core values, talents, and passions are, design a career or business that will incorporate those values on a day-to-day basis. If your core values drive your business, life will be more fulfilling, and success will come much easier. People always do best what they love to do the most. We will discuss this more in the next step toward your ultimate success.

Guided Meditation: Introduction to *Stillness*

A CD of this meditation is available from Amazon.com and other retail outlets.

Find a place where you will not be observed or disturbed.
Sit up straight in a comfortable position.
Close your eyes.
Allow yourself to breathe naturally. Take breath in. Let breath out.

Now take a deep cleansing breath in, through your nose if possible. Notice the rise and fall of your chest and abdomen. Notice the sense of chill as the cool air passes through your nostrils. Blow it all out, pushing up with your diaphragm to empty your lungs completely. Take a second cleansing breath to rejuvenate your lungs with fresh air.

Take a few upper breaths, focusing on pushing the air into the chest portion of your lungs. Take your fingertips and touch your heart. Feel your chest move up and down as you take each breath. Breathe in, through your nose if possible, and out through your mouth. If you can't breathe that way, don't worry. That technique is just a way to help take your mind off other things and concentrate on your breath.

Now take a few lower breaths, focusing on pushing air as deeply into your abdomen as possible. Again, breathe in, through your nose if possible, and out through your mouth. As you inhale, imagine yourself breathing in positive energy. As you exhale, imagine yourself breathing out negative energy. Say to yourself:

> *Breathe in peace; breathe out anxiety.*
> *Breathe in faith; breathe out doubt.*
> *Breathe in love; breathe out indifference.*

Breathe in hope; breathe out despair.
Breathe in confidence; breathe out timidity.

Balance your breathing.

Empty your mind of feelings of stress or anxiety. Thoughts about problems at work or home may rush in at this point. That's normal. Don't fight the thoughts. Just acknowledge them and let them slip away.

Relax your body. Focus on your head. Recognize any tension in your scalp, face, or jaw. Will each area to relax. Let your jaw slip down slightly into a relaxed position. Now focus on your neck and shoulders. Again, recognize any tension and will each area to relax. Repeat this relaxation technique for your arms and chest. As you focus on your diaphragm, you may notice your breathing change a bit. You may begin to breathe a little more deeply and regularly as if asleep. Continue the technique, moving down your body until you reach your toes. Take a moment to realize that you are fully relaxed.

As before, focus on your breath. Empty yourself of other thoughts. Notice your sense of peace. Notice your awareness of sounds around you. Are there other feelings or sensations? Do you find yourself stretching or yawning? Are there other manifestations of tension release? Whatever your body wants to do in this state is okay. Just let yourself relax.

Now take a deep breath and let it all out. Again.

If positive thoughts came to you in your meditative state, you may want to write down some notes. If nothing came to you, that's fine, we're just getting started here.

Notes from Your Guided Meditation

_____

_____

_____

_____

_____

_____

_____

_____

_____

_____

_____

_____

CHAPTER 2

What Goals Will Support Your Values, Talents, and Passions?

Part of the issue of achievement is to be able to set realistic goals, but that's one of the hardest things to do because you don't always know exactly where you're going, and you shouldn't.
- George Lucas

We've uncovered your true core values, underlying talents, and passions. It's often difficult to see our values, talents, and passions because the necessities of life take up all our mental awareness. In the same way, it's often difficult to choose the goals that will support our true core values. This is especially true of people who are exceptionally smart or talented. They enjoy so many activities and are good at so many projects, that they have a hard time focusing on one or two objectives so they can excel and be successful.

The weekend warrior is mediocre at a dozen different sports. Olympians have focused their attention and training so they are #1 in their field. Which would you rather be, the weekend warrior or the Olympian?

Are You Serious About Your Goals?

What you get by achieving your goals is not as important as what you become by achieving your goals.
- Henry David Thoreau

Outline a new set of goals. Pursue them and watch your life change forever. Whether it changes for the better or for the worse, depends on the goals you set for yourself.

Your goals are the waypoints along the road to your ultimate life vision. At this point in the process, you should be developing a picture of what you really want out of life. Now make what you want tangible. Put it on paper. Make it tangible. Make it real.

Honestly, are other people setting your goals for you? Your parents? Your teachers? Your religious leaders? Your boss? Your circle of friends? Your spouse?

Everything changes today. Today is the day you take control of your life and map your own future. Goal setting is exciting and invigorating - but only if you set the goals yourself.

You've seen all the self-help books devoted to goal setting. Some are quite good. Others merely rehash what everyone intuitively knows about goals. Their only purpose is to present the same material with a new twist on the accepted acronym. Most agree that goals need to be **SMART** (**S**imple - **M**easureable - **A**chievable - **R**ealistic - **T**imeframe) or (**S**pecific - **M**easureable - **A**ttainable - **R**elevant - **T**imely). Someone did one better and came up with **SMARTER** goals, the aforementioned plus **E**valuate and **R**edo.

Here is my spin on the acronym. Goals need to be **S**pecific, **M**otivating, **A**ccountable, **R**ealistic, and **T**ough.

Specific
Research has demonstrated that goals need to be specific and clearly understood to be effective. If you are in sales

and your goal is to go over your quota this quarter, you will likely hit quota plus one dollar. You might not even do that. "Over" is just too general a concept to drive many individuals. If you set a goal to beat your quota by 10%, that's more specific. It gives you a clearer goal to reach for.

Motivating

Goals must be motivating. Common sense tells us that we have to be motivated to get ourselves out of bed an hour early to study for the exam, run a mile before breakfast, or whatever lifestyle change is needed to accomplish our goal. Virtually all goals require a lifestyle change. That's where well-intentioned goals often fall apart. Sure, many of us would like to lose some weight. If your goal of loosing ten pounds doesn't motivate you as much as having a chocolate chip brownie hot fudge sundae, then you may as well just go out and buy a bigger shirt. So just how motivating are your goals?

Accountable

Accountability is a popular catchword in the coaching world. What's it all about? Why is it such an important aspect of achieving your goals?

Dr. Gail Matthews conducted a study on goal setting with 267 volunteer participants.[5] They were separated into five groups.

Group 1 had mental, but unwritten goals.

Group 2 had written goals.

Group 3 had written goals with a plan of action.

Group 4 had written goals, a plan of action, and told other people about their goals.

Group 5 had written goals, a plan of action, and an accountability partner to whom they made weekly progress reports.

Those who were in Group 5 outperformed all other groups and were almost twice as likely to fulfill their goals as those in Group 1.

Friends, mentors, or professional life or business coaches make great accountability partners. Perhaps there is someone who would be willing to be a mutual accountability partner. Each of you will be accountable to the other. The bottom line is if you want to achieve your goal, have an accountability partner. Set up a regularly scheduled time to discuss your progress toward your goals.

Realistic

Isn't every goal realistic if you want it bad enough? Not if it is unreachable. But don't sell yourself short either. If you want to be president of the United States, that's a realistic goal - unless you were born in Canada. You would have to change the Constitution of the United States to become president, and that would probably make the goal of becoming president unrealistic. If you want to be a professional basketball player, that's a realistic goal - unless you're 60 years old and 5 foot 2. The rule of thumb is, unless there is a physical or legal limitation preventing you from reaching your goal, go for it!

Tough

Finally, you want to have tough goals. Set the bar high. If your goals don't challenge as well as motivate you to perform at a higher level than you are now, they're worthless. Setting a goal to be mediocre just doesn't jazz anyone.

A tough goal forces you to focus on it and work for it.

Every two years, thousands of young people watch the Olympic Games and set a goal to participate in the next

Olympic Games in four years. The vast majority don't achieve their goal. However, everyone who made that goal became a better athlete and better person to the extent they truly pursued their goal.

You may not reach your goal, but you will be better for having tried. Becoming a better you is a valuable part of your success formula.

But you thought the "T" stood for timeliness?
In my view, the timeframe for completion of a goal is not part of the goal itself, but part of the plan of action. We'll discuss the plan of action in Chapter 7. For now, it's okay for you to relax regarding how long it takes you to accomplish a goal. I have known many goal setters in my life, and few have achieved their goal in their initial timeframe.

You are one decision away from changing your life forever.

Your "I Want" List is More Than a Pipe Dream

Map out your future, but do it in pencil.
- Jon Bon Jovi

Make a list of potential goals. Call it the "I want" list. These can be material objects like a new home, car, or boat. They can be achievements like a new job, promotion, or ideal weight. They can be spiritual like more family time or volunteering at a homeless shelter. Go ahead and list everything you think of that you would like to have, achieve, or become. Do not leave anything off because it seems unattainable or silly. Listing some wild ideas may lead you to something very powerful. We'll clean up the list later.

Why Categorize Your Goals?

To come up with a large list of potential goals, I find it easiest to think in terms of categories.

Try this: Ask yourself, "What do I want to become, possess, or accomplish in each area of my life?" Too often, we think in general terms and become fixated on whatever issue is disturbing us at the moment. It may be career, financial, or family. By forcing yourself to come up with at least potential goals in areas like hobbies or vacations, you are able to develop a much more comprehensive picture of what you want to accomplish in life. You may even come up with a few surprises.

My "I Want" List

Write 10 things you want to become, possess, accomplish in each area of your life.

Career/Business

1. _____

2. _____

3. _____

4. _____

5. _____

6. _____

7. _____

8. _____

9. _____

10. _____

Family/Relationship

1. _____

2. _____

3. _____

4. _____

5. _____

6. _____

7. _____

8. _____

9. _____

10. _____

Spiritual

1 _____

2. _____

3. _____

4. _____

5. _____

6. _____

7. _____

8. _____

9. _____

10. _____

Financial

1. _____

2. _____

3. _____

4. _____

5. _____

6. _____

7. _____

8. _____

9. _____

10. _____

Recreation/Hobbies

1. _____

42

2. _____

3. _____

4. _____

5. _____

6. _____

7. _____

8. _____

9. _____

10. _____

Possessions

1. _____

2. _____

3. _____

4. _____

5. _____

6. _____

7. _____

8. _____

9. _____

10. _____

Vacation/Travel

1. _____
2. _____
3. _____
4. _____
5. _____
6. _____
7. _____
8. _____
9. _____
10. _____

Social

1. _____
2. _____
3. _____
4. _____
5. _____
6. _____

7. _____

8. _____

9. _____

10. _____

Health

1. _____

2. _____

3. _____

4. _____

5. _____

6. _____

7. _____

8. _____

9. _____

10. _____

Education/Learning

1. _____

2. _____

3. _____

4. _____

5. _____

6. _____

7. _____

8. _____

9. _____

10. _____

Other: _____

1. _____

2. _____

3. _____

4. _____

5. _____

6. _____

7. _____

8. _____

9. _____

10. _____

But What are Your Ultimate Goals?

Not only do your goals need to support your core values, your core values need to support your goals. For example, perhaps one of your core values is family. You want to spend as much time with your family as possible and develop true closeness. However, one of the things you have always wanted to do is sail around the world solo. You may as well drop the world cruise because your inner self will not let you accomplish it. It's contrary to your core value of family. Of course, you can also alter your goal to being able to afford to take your whole family on a two-week cruise once a year. Now that's a goal your inner self can get behind and support.

Now, go back, look over the list, and ask yourself, "Which of these really support my true core values?" Put a checkmark by the ones that would really support your core values. That should knock out about a third of your list.

A Word about Your Inner Self

I think the idea that you know your inner self is the first ingredient for success.
- Whoopi Goldberg

Your core values reside in your inner self, the true YOU. It's similar to what Freud called the "super-ego." It's that part of you that's mostly unconscious. It operates like your conscience. The super-ego serves to support or restrict the desires of the ego. It manifests in a sense of purpose or a destiny. It overrides pleasure and pain drives to accomplish something greater. It is what makes an athlete keep going after he or she is exhausted. It gives courage to a soldier who risks his life to save others.

Deep within you is a YOU. If you're like most people in this fast-paced, high-stress, work-hard-to-get-ahead world, you don't get in touch with your true YOU very often.

A sociologist once described man as an onion. Skin after skin is peeled away only to reveal another skin. There is a work skin, a parent skin, a spouse skin, a child of aging parents skin, and so forth. After you have peeled away all the skins, you have nothing. I disagree.

Yes, we adjust to fit into different situations and roles, but deep within us is a true self. As I mentioned earlier, the true you comes out during periods of great stress or great joy.

We ignore our true self at our peril. Many people take jobs because they think they can make a lot of money at them, but never enjoy success. That's because they did not choose careers that support their inner self or their core values. Their inner self will not *allow* them to succeed. Their inner self is constantly trying to draw them out of their current job into a different job or career that will support their core values.

You have probably known people who seem to change jobs or careers every 10 years or so. Others work in the same career for 30 years but never receive satisfaction from it. If either of these describes you, then you are reading the right book.

Get in touch with your inner self. Identify your core values. Then set goals that will take you where you truly want to go.

Go back to your list, but this time identify those goals that are well supported by your innate talents and abilities. It's very difficult to succeed if you're not happy with who you are. Part of being happy with who you are is to celebrate your own talents and abilities. If you really prefer to work alone (soloist), don't beat yourself up for not being a good team player. Just focus on goals that are accomplished best by individual effort. Focusing on which goals are best supported by your innate talents and abilities should further reduce your list of potential goals.

Many people have difficulty doing a realistic self-appraisal. This is a great place for a good consultant, mentor, or coach to provide some useful feedback. Humans are notoriously poor at self-assessment. There is no substitute for an honest reflection on our strengths and weaknesses from a professional who has our best interest at heart. Find a coach or mentor who will provide a look at yourself from a different set of eyes.

Avoid the lure of imagining yourself the underdog who overcomes all odds to become the hero. Inspirational stories and movies tend to idolize people who overcame great adversity to achieve goals everyone thought was impossible to them. While these stories are remarkable and inspiring, it is far more practical to pursue goals that are supported by your innate talents and abilities. Life will be more enjoyable if your pursuit of excellence is in areas that you are naturally good at. You will wow the world and yourself with your accomplishments.

Now It's Time to Get Excited!

Ask yourself, "Which of the remaining "I Wants" really excite me?"

What really jazzes you from the list? When you read it, do you feel giddy? Do you get excited imagining actually accomplishing certain specific goals? Draw a circle around them Focus on these goals.

Imagine You Just Won the Lottery

Have you ever dreamed about winning the lottery? Even if wealth is not one of your core values, stay with me. I think everyone can learn something important about himself or herself through this exercise.

Sit back and imagine you have more money than you can spend. If you can spend a lot, just imagine even more. Your time is your own. You can do whatever you want. You can buy whatever you want. This can be a difficult exercise for many people. We don't want to seem so "selfish" as to have all that money to spend on ourselves. However, remember: This is just an exercise. It is not real life. So indulge yourself. What would you do? What would you buy? With whom would you spend your time? Do not imagine just a day, but imagine weeks, months, and even years of having everything you could possibly want and doing everything you've ever dreamed of.

The reason you need to extend the time frame for this exercise is that many people begin their lottery-winning daydream by imagining some sort of extended vacation. They lounge around on a beach, reading good books, going fishing, or just doing nothing while being pampered at a spa or resort. However, if you can imagine moving from hot tub to massage table every day for a year, at some point you will think, "This is getting boring." You want to do something that matters to someone, to make some kind of difference in the world. Now you're getting down to your inner self.

If you did not have to worry about making money to pay the bills or keep a roof over your family's heads, what would you be doing? What is it you would do regardless of whether or not you were being paid to do it? Now you are probably looking at a goal that supports your true core values.

Another way to find what you truly want to do is to ask yourself the question, "If all jobs paid the same, what would I do for a living?" Many of us pursue accidental careers. We got a job, were promoted, and found ourselves locked into a career we never intended. Others pursue careers they think will be profitable, whether or not they enjoy what they do.

I am not suggesting you try to turn your hobby into a business. Too often, hobbies make poor businesses. Even if they are lucrative, they cease to be fun once they change from being a hobby into being a job. What I am suggesting is that you pursue a business or vocation:
1. That supports your core values
2. For which you have natural talents and abilities
3. You can be passionate about

When those criteria are met, your endeavor will be enjoyable and fulfilling.

Proficiency follows passion. You will naturally be good at doing what you enjoy because it will be a pleasure to commit the time and energy needed to develop skill. If you enjoy your work and do it well, you will find advancement and financial rewards will soon follow.

What About Other Areas of Your Life?

These principles apply not just to business and career goals, but also to every area of your life. They should be considered when outlining any goals, whether you're choosing a college major, choosing a life partner, or planning for retirement.

When considering a life partner, it's always best to choose someone who shares your core values, has complimentary talents and abilities, and about whom you are very passionate.

Selecting a college major is much the same as selecting a career. I am saddened by how many students get degrees in something they truly enjoy, and then take the first job available after they graduate. That may be because they majored in their hobby, not in a field that truly supported their core values, utilized their innate talents and abilities, and about which they were truly passionate.

Retirement is not just about having enough savings in your retirement account to make ends meet after the paychecks stop. A host of new choices greets every retiree. Where do you want to live? How are you going to maintain an income after retirement? Should you pursue a retirement career? Once again, it is important to take into account your core values, innate talents, and true passions.

Can You Narrow Your Goals Even More?

Did the preceding exercises leave you with a short list of goals? It is okay to have 100 or more goals, but since you can only focus on one to three goals at a time - the fewer, the better. Otherwise, you will not be able to give any goal the attention it needs to be fully accomplished. Perhaps both exercises narrowed the field down to a single goal. That's great. Focus on that one. Perhaps each exercise narrowed down to a different goal. Okay, now you have two goals to focus on.

If you have more than three goals, continue to narrow them down. Choose which one, two, or three goals truly support your core values. Which one, two, or three goals will your inner self push you to accomplish? These are your ultimate goals. They are not ultimate in the sense of absolute and static. Your goals will change as your circumstances change. Your goals may also change as your understanding grows. Remember, these are *your* goals. If you choose goals that will fulfill someone else's dream, your inner self will not allow you to accomplish them.

If you are still having difficulty focusing on one to three goals, don't worry. We'll talk about prioritizing goals in a later chapter.

My Ultimate Goals

My first goal is:

_____

The reason I have made this my primary goal is:

_____

I know my inner self will support this goal because:

_____

My second goal is:

_____

This goal is important to me because:

_____

I know my inner self will support this goal because:

_____

My third goal is:

_____

This goal is important to me because:

_____

I know my inner self will support this goal because:

_____

Printable worksheets can be downloaded from
WhereDoIGoFromHere.net

Why Measure Your Progress?

When you were young, your parents may have marked the progress of your physical growth on a wall or door lintel. You waited with anticipation before each measurement. You were filled with pride to see how you had grown. The same is true of measuring your progress toward your goal.

Take a mental self-assessment at 30-, 60-, and 90-day marks. Are you closer to the ideal YOU than you were in the beginning? Are you making more money? Are you losing weight? Are your friends and coworkers treating you differently? Are people coming to you for advice and counsel? Are you treating your family and associates differently?

Progress may seem slow at first. But remember that it took years to get you to the place you are now. It may take some time to get on your true track.

In the following chart, note your starting point in relation to your goal. For example, if your goal is an ideal weight, your starting point would be your current weight. Your goal would be your ideal weight. Monitor your progress at the 30, 60, and 90-day points.

55

Progress Chart

Starting Point	Goal	30 Day Progress	60 Day Progress	90 Day Progress

Progress Chart

Overcome Resistance to Your Goals

Success is not final, failure is not fatal: it is the courage to continue that counts.
- Winston Churchill

Imagine you lived in a giant protective bubble. This bubble includes your family, your home, your job, your friends, your hobbies, and even your favorite TV shows. This protective bubble is called your "comfort zone." You are familiar with everything in your comfort zone, and that gives you a sense of comfort, even if it's false. You have begun recognizing trouble in your bubble. Perhaps it's a dead-end job. Perhaps it's insufficient finances to make ends meet. You want to make changes in your life, so you set goals. But your goals lie outside of your comfort bubble. To accomplish your goal you must expand your bubble so that it includes your goal. In other words, it's time to make changes in your life or yourself so you're comfortable with the steps needed to achieve your goal.

You make goals because you want something you don't have. In other words, they are outside of your current reality. They can be:
- Material
- Professional
- Personal
- Spiritual

Because your goal is outside of your current reality, you must make some changes to achieve it. Some of those changes may be uncomfortable or even frightening. Albert Einstein once said, "You can't solve a problem with the same thinking you used to create it." To accomplish your goals you will need to change your thinking and expand your comfort zone.

Here are some steps you may need to take to expand your comfort zone.

- Miss some TV shows.
- Speak with people you might otherwise ignore.
- Take risks with people you admire.
- Tell friends you're opening a new business. (Face your fear of failure.)
- Ask people if they want to order from you. (Face your fear of rejection.)
- Enroll in an online study course to get a new degree.
- Learn to speak publicly.
- Become comfortable calling on or socializing with a higher level of management.
- Learn to write effectively.

What happens when you start to expand your comfort zone? It is actually similar to exercising and stretching previously unused muscles. You start to feel discomfort, even pain.

What happens when you feel uncomfortable? You want to return to your original comfort bubble.

When that happens, two possibilities present themselves.

1. Reduce the goal to something that fits within your current comfort zone.

or,

2. Change your attitude.

What keeps you from moving forward? It's not the lack of opportunity, the lack of funding, or the lack of the correct degree. All those things can be created or acquired if you're sufficiently motivated. Your attitude keeps you where you are. Change your attitude and you can expand your comfort zone.

Attitudes can be very stubborn, especially if we have held onto them for a long time. Here are three exercises that will help you change your attitude.

1. Affirmations. Take a realistic look at any attitudes that are holding you back. Write affirmations that will engender a new attitude. Read them daily. If possible, read them aloud several times a day.

2. Visualization. Picture yourself having accomplished your goal. Write it out using emotional language. Describe your feelings at having accomplished your goal. Describe sights, sounds, and smells of your new life. Read your vision daily.

3. Practice. Pretend you're not afraid and just do it. As you stretch yourself, the barriers of your old bubble will vanish as phantasms.

We will discuss affirmations and visualization in more detail soon.

Values Meditation

A CD of this meditation is available from Amazon.com and other retail outlets.

The following technique is a simple way to help you see who you can be. We all had some rocky spots in our growing-up years. I never met the person with a perfect childhood. This exercise allows you to create a perfect model in your imagination. It can help you get past some of the defenses you built to protect yourself and discover a "you" full of possibilities and potential.

Find a place where you will not be observed or disturbed.

Sit up straight in a comfortable position.

Close your eyes.

Allow yourself to breathe naturally. Take breath in. Let breath out.

Now take a deep cleansing breath in through your nose, if possible. Notice the rise and fall of your chest and abdomen. Notice the sense of chill as the cool air passes through your nostrils. Blow it all out, pushing up with your diaphragm to empty your lungs completely. Take a second cleansing breath to rejuvenate your lungs with fresh air.

Take a few upper breaths, focusing on pushing the air into the chest portion of your lungs. Take your fingertips and touch your heart. Feel your chest move up and down as you take each breath. Breathe in, through your nose if possible, and out through your mouth. If you can't breathe that way, don't worry. That technique is just a way to help take your mind off other things and concentrate on your breath.

Now take a few lower breaths, focusing on pushing air as deeply into your abdomen as possible. Again, breathe in, through your nose if possible, and out through your mouth. As you inhale, imagine yourself breathing in positive energy. As you exhale, imagine yourself breathing out negative energy. Say to yourself:

> *Breathe in peace; breathe out anxiety.*
> *Breathe in faith; breathe out doubt.*
> *Breathe in love; breathe out indifference.*
> *Breathe in hope; breathe out despair.*
> *Breathe in confidence; breathe out timidity.*

Empty your mind of feelings of stress or anxiety. Thoughts about problems at work or home may rush in at this point. That's normal. Don't fight the thoughts. Just acknowledge them and let them slip away.

Relax your body. Focus on your head. Recognize any tension in your scalp, face, or jaw. Will each area to relax. Let your jaw slip down slightly into a relaxed position. Now focus on your neck and shoulders. Again, recognize any tension and will each area to relax. Repeat this relaxation technique for your arms and chest. As you focus on your diaphragm, your breathing may alter a bit. You may begin to breathe a little more deeply and regularly as if asleep. Continue the technique, moving down your body until you reach your toes. Take a moment to realize that you are fully relaxed.

Imagine yourself as a child in a very happy state. This could be a memory from your own childhood but it doesn't have to be. If you have a very happy memory or a very happy place, that's fine. You can use it as a springboard into this exercise. If not, you can create your own imaginary time and place.

Imagine yourself as a happy, secure, and peaceful child. There are loving and supportive adults around. There is no judgment here, only loving support. Think about this child. What do you like about this child? Is the child you? Is this the childhood you wish you had? Think about the adults. What makes these adults special? What qualities do they possess that you want this child to be aware of?

Fast-forward the scene. The child is now a young teen. The child is confident and excited about growing up. What does this teenager want to be when he or she grows up? What does he or she want to be like? Think of the qualities this teenager should be developing over the next ten years.

Fast forward again. The teenager is now in his or her mid-twenties, just starting out on his or her own life. What qualities does this young adult have? Personality? Work ethic? Family life? Goals? Morals? Spirituality?

Now take a deep breath and let it all out. Again.

Now take some notes. What did you learn about yourself and your values as you watched this child grow up? What qualities or values did you see in the child, teen, or young adult that you identified with as your own values, or values you would like to develop as your own? Write them down and take time to reflect on them.

Notes from Your Guided Meditation

_____

_____

_____

_____

_____

_____

_____

_____

_____

_____

_____

_____

_____

CHAPTER 3

What Will Your Life Look Like After You Have Accomplished Your Goals?

Of course I'm ambitious. What's wrong with that?
Otherwise you sleep all day.
- Ringo Starr

Can the three ultimate goals you wrote in Chapter 2 combine to form one comprehensive life vision? Where will you live? Can you describe your home? Who will you be living with? What kind of car will you drive? Will you have a job? Will you be self-employed? What kind of investments will you have? Where will you be going on vacation? Who will you be helping and how? The answers to these questions and others that might come to mind make up your life vision. It's where you want to end up after all is said and done. Your life vision can have enormous power to motivate you when times get hard and accomplishing your goals seems not worth the effort.

Accomplishing your goals is going to take discipline and hard work. There will be times you may want to quit. When that happens, the only thing that will keep you going is the vision of your life after you have accomplished your goals. Your vision is what all the hard work is for.

Visualization is not Daydreaming

The self-help genre garners a lot of hype and skepticism about meditation and visualization. That's because the case for meditation and visualization, often associated with the so-called law of attraction, has sometimes been overstated. You may have heard some authors describe visualization as some sort of magical daydream. It would be nice if we could just imagine whatever we want, toss it out to the universe, and have the universe do all the work for us. I have even heard some tout that bad visualization can attract car accidents and natural disasters.

Let me state clearly that visualization isn't magic. You don't get a million dollars in your bank account by just thinking about it. Neither do you attract a car accident by having negative thoughts. You may attract one by driving tired or distracted, but not by having bad self talk or a bad visualization model. I grew up in the East Texas Bible belt where someone was always telling me if I had the right kind of faith, good things would happen to me. If bad things happened, I just didn't have enough faith. That's a bunch of baloney. Much of what I hear about self talk, meditation, visualization, and the law of attraction is the same old snake oil with a new label.

Some claim the law of attraction is the key to success in business, but if you really want to succeed in business, you need a good business plan, dynamite marketing, great customer service, and a lot of hard work. Meditation and visualization have their place; one could even argue they are essential. Nevertheless, they are no substitute for planning and hard work.

Now that I've begun this chapter with an overdone caveat, let's talk about what is real and practical about meditation, visualization, and the practice of *Stillness*.

How Can You Stay Focused?

Your vision will become clear only when you can look into your own heart. Who looks outside, dreams; who looks inside, awakes.
- Carl Jung

Laura was a writer who, like many writers, had difficulty carrying a project to its completion. As with many talented people, she had so many things to say and so many things to write about, it was too easy to switch from one project to the next without ever finishing one. To keep her on track, she took up the practice of daily visualization. Each day she sat comfortably and relaxed with some deep-breathing exercises. She looked into her empty hands and visualized her finished book. She imagined the cover with her chosen illustrations and her name in bold print. She now consults with other authors, helping them through the long road to publishing.[6]

You will never reach your goal unless you keep it in your mind's eye. There are so many opportunities in life, so many distractions, so many chances to turn aside from your chosen path, that it's difficult to steer a steady course to your desired destination. If you want to be successful, you must stay focused.

Visualize your ultimate goal. Regularly imagine the vision of your life. Play it like a movie in your mind's eye. Your vision will help you reject distractions and stay on track.

What Will Keep You Motivated?

Shortly after Jim Carrey arrived in Los Angeles to initiate his acting career, he wrote himself a check for $10,000,000. In the memo, he noted, "For acting services rendered." He post-dated the check Thanksgiving, 1995 and carried the check in his wallet for years until it was worn and faded. The check was a physical representation of a dream. It gave substance to the intangible. When his father passed away in 1994, Jim placed the tattered check into his father's casket because his father had instilled in Jim the courage to pursue his dream. Then, just before Thanksgiving 1995, Jim received a contract offer to star in the movie, *Dumb and Dumber*. The offer on the contract was $10,000,000.

Muhammad Ali once said, "I hated every minute of training. But I said to myself, 'Don't quit. Suffer now, and live the rest of your life as a champion.'" [7] If your life vision is strong and enticing, it will provide you with the motivation to keep pressing ahead when you feel like quitting. No goal worth achieving is easy. Set your mind and your heart on your vision, because your vision is why you're working so hard to achieve your goals.

How Can You Optimize Your Performance?

Jack Nicklaus, one of the greatest golfers of all time said, "I never hit a shot, not even in practice, without having a very sharp, in-focus picture of it in my head. First, I see the ball where I want it to finish, nice, white, and sitting up high on the bright green grass. Then the scene quickly changes, and I see the ball going there; its path, trajectory, and shape, even its behavior on landing. Then there is a sort of fade-out, and the next scene shows me making the kind of swing that will turn the previous images into reality." [8] Sports greats have long used visualization to improve their performance.

Whatever your field of endeavor, whether sales, management, construction, or the arts, visualization of both your end product and your process will always improve your performance.

Big Goals Require a Big Vision

You are not here merely to make a living. You are here in order to enable the world to live more amply, with greater vision, with a finer spirit of hope and achievement. You are here to enrich the world, and you impoverish yourself if you forget the errand.
- Woodrow Wilson

Daily Muhammad Ali visualized being the heavy weight champion of the world. He imagined his opponents as destined for defeat. He often spoke of these visualizations as the driving motivation to keep him training at 100% on days he just didn't feel like it.[9]

The bigger your goal, the bigger your vision needs to be to motivate you and keep you inspired to accomplish it. Ask yourself why you want to achieve your goal. If your goal is to become a manager at the place where you work, what is it about being a manager that will motivate you to do what it takes to become a manager? Is your goal to become the top sales person in your organization? The question is, "Why?" Is it for the money? The prestige? The recognition? There is no wrong answer here. It's just important to know the personal, inspiring reason for your goal, so you can keep yourself motivated to whatever it takes to reach your goal. Just remember: If your vision is too small, so will your effort be.

What Do You Really Want?

Zig Ziglar is famous for saying, "Every year thousands of people go out and buy one-quarter-inch drill bits, but not one of them wanted a one-quarter-inch drill bit. They all wanted one-quarter-inch holes."

Looking past the externals of the position or achievement, what is it you truly want? What is it you are working toward?

It is common for many people to have some sort of financial goals, but what they really want is not money. They really want something else that having money provides for them. It may be a bigger house. Better education for the kids. The freedom to travel. Or perhaps they're motivated by intangibles like security, confidence, recognition, freedom from worrying about money, or even the ability to give more to those in need.

What is it that you really want? What will motivate you to do what it takes to get it?

Write it Out - Make it Real

All successful people men and women are big dreamers. They imagine what their future could be, ideal in every respect, and then they work every day toward their distant vision, that goal or purpose.
- Brian Tracy

Jack was a college student who wanted to graduate valedictorian of his class. He asked his mother to sew a wall hanging with a big "V" on it. Every day for four years, he looked at that wall hanging and took a moment to think about what it would feel like to be named valedictorian of his graduating class. He thought about what he would say in his speech. He imagined the applause. Then, he went to class focused on making the grades necessary to be valedictorian. Sure enough, when his class graduated, Jack was named valedictorian. Only then did he tell all his friends what the wall hanging was all about. For four years, they had questioned him. Now they all understood.

Take a moment to write out your ideal day in your ideal life. Get out your notebook or daily journal and describe it in as much detail as you can. Imagine your feelings about having accomplished your goals. Where are you? Who are you with? What kind of work are you doing? What do you do to relax? Do you travel? If so, where?

You don't have to be a novelist to write a detailed description of something you hold deeply in your heart. As you picture your life after you have achieved your goals, ask yourself, "What do I see?" and "What do I hear" and "What do I smell?" and "What do I feel?" If your goal is to make enough money to give your children the best education available, imagine yourself sitting in the audience with other parents at an Ivy League college. Feel the enthusiasm. Hear the applause. Note the pride swelling up inside of you.

The subconscious thinks in terms of symbols and images. What we are doing here is implanting your goal into your subconscious. The more vivid the image you implant into your subconscious, the harder your subconscious will work to make that image a reality.

Take time everyday to read your vision and imagine your life after you have achieved your goals. Give your subconscious a destination, and it will find a way to get there.

Emotion Empowers Your Vision

Brain power improves by brain use, just as our bodily strength grows with exercise.
- A. N. Wilson

There is power in emotional links, and you want all the power you can muster. Several studies have shown that memory is closely linked to emotion. If you experience deep emotion during an event, you will remember it forever. If you're a parent, you probably remember in vivid detail the events and surroundings related to the birth of your children. You can also probably describe in detail the room you were in and what you were doing when you heard about the terrorist attacks of 9-11.

When describing your life vision, create a memory in advance. Describe what you feel when you realize the accomplishment of your goals. Your brain builds neuro-pathways so that often-repeated thoughts, actions, and emotions travel more quickly though your nervous system than new thoughts, actions, or emotions.

Martial artists and other athletes develop what they call "muscle memory." A punch is blocked and a counter punch is thrown without conscious thought. The gymnast approaches the rings to perform a program he has practiced a thousand times. He doesn't have to tell his body what to do. He performs the routine automatically from "muscle memory."

We experience the same phenomena every day. A compliment triggers an automated response. We smile, perhaps blush a little. We say, "Thank you." An insult, especially one we are particularly tired of hearing, triggers a different response.

Just as an athlete trains his body to have "muscle memory," you can train yourself to have a desired emotional response to a preset trigger. The salesperson can preset an emotional response of enthusiasm and excitement to the act of picking up the phone to make a cold call. The competitor can preset the excitement of victory to the opening of any competition.

You can also preset strong emotions to your life vision.

Take a moment to think of the most exciting and joyful experience of your life. You will probably begin feeling the same emotions all over again. You may begin to smile or laugh. Now picture the fulfillment of your life vision. Mentally attach those feelings to your vision. Feel the excitement and joy of having fulfilled your life vision. You may need to repeat this exercise the first few times you read your vision. Soon you'll discover that the emotions will come naturally and quickly. This emotional preset can keep you moving toward your goal when challenges seem insurmountable.

If the reason why you want your goal is strong enough, what it takes to achieve it is never too hard.

Life Vision Worksheet

Review your three ultimate goals. Restate them as needed to make sure their fulfillment creates the life of your dreams.

In the following exercise, write a detailed vision for each of your top three goals. Later you will combine them to make a comprehensive life vision.

Vision Worksheet #1

Restate your first goal.

_____

Write a picture of your life after you have achieved your goal.

_____

Name at least three things you see in your vision.

_____

Name at least one smell that's present.

_____

What sounds do you hear?

_____

Who is present with you?

_____

What emotions do you feel?

_____

Describe your current motivation to reach your goal and make this vision real.

_____

Vision Worksheet #2

Restate your second goal.

_____

Write a picture of your life after you have achieved your goal.

_____

Name at least three things you see in your vision.

_____

Name at least one smell that's present.

_____

What sounds do you hear?

_____

Who is present with you?

_____

What emotions do you feel?

_____

Describe your current motivation to reach your goal and make this vision real.

_____

Vision Worksheet #3

Restate your third goal.

_____

Write a picture of your life after you have achieved your goal.

_____

Name at least three things you see in your vision.

_____

Name at least one smell that's present.

_____

What sounds do you hear?

_____

Who is present with you?

_____

What emotions do you feel?

_____

Describe your current motivation to reach your goal and make this vision real.

_____

Life Vision

Use your three vision worksheets to write a composite life vision. Remember to address the following:

1. Where are you?
2. Who are you with?
3. What are you doing?
4. When have you achieved this vision?
5. Why have you committed your life to the fulfillment of this vision?

_____

_____

_____

_____

_____

_____

_____

_____

_____

Keep your vision in front of you. It's the key to your motivation. Take time each day to imagine what it is you're working toward.

Set aside time at the beginning and end of each day to:
- Read your vision.
- Create a mental picture of your life after you have reached your goals.
- Imagine the sights, smells and other sensory input.
- Feel the emotions of joy and elation that come from achieving your goals.

Life Vision Meditation

A CD of this meditation is available from Amazon.com and other retail outlets.

With the Life Vision you just wrote in front of you, do the following meditation:

Find a place where you will not be observed or disturbed.

Sit up straight in a comfortable position.

Close your eyes.

Allow yourself to breathe naturally. Take breath in. Let breath out.

Now take a deep cleansing breath in through your nose, if possible. Notice the rise and fall of your chest and abdomen. Notice the sense of chill as the cool air passes through your nostrils. Blow it all out, pushing up with your diaphragm to empty your lungs completely. Take a second cleansing breath to rejuvenate your lungs with fresh air.

Take a few upper breaths, focusing on pushing the air into the chest portion of your lungs. Take your fingertips and touch your heart. Feel your chest move up and down as you take your breath. Breathe in, through your nose if possible, and out through your mouth. If you can't breathe that way, don't worry. That technique is just a way to help take your mind off other things and concentrate on your breath.

Now take a few lower breaths, focusing on pushing air as deeply into your abdomen as possible. Again, breathe in, through your nose if possible, and out through your mouth. As you inhale, imagine yourself breathing in positive

energy. As you exhale, imagine yourself breathing out negative energy. Say to yourself:

Breathe in peace; breathe out anxiety.
Breathe in faith; breathe out doubt.
Breathe in love; breathe out indifference.
Breathe in hope; breathe out despair.
Breathe in confidence; breathe out timidity.

Empty your mind of feelings of stress or anxiety. Thoughts about problems at work or home may rush in at this point. That's normal. Don't fight the thoughts. Just acknowledge them and let them slip away.

Relax your body. Focus on your head. Recognize any tension in your scalp, face, or jaw. Will each area to relax. Let your jaw slip down slightly into a relaxed position. Now focus on your neck and shoulders. Again, recognize any tension and will each area to relax. Repeat this relaxation technique for your arms and chest. As you focus on your diaphragm, your breathing may alter a bit. You may begin to breathe a little more deeply and regularly as if asleep. Continue the technique, moving down your body until you reach your toes. Take a moment to realize that you are fully relaxed.

In your mind's eye, picture your life the way you want it to be.

When is it? Is it a month from now? A year from now? Ten years from now?

Where are you? Are you in a home or an office? What does it look like?

Who are you with? Are you with family? Friends? Coworkers?

What are you doing? What is your job or endeavor? What do you enjoy most about this job or endeavor?

How did you get to this point in your life? What did you do? Whom did you do it with? Was the effort hard? Was the effort worth it?

Why did you do whatever it took to get to this point in your life? Was it for yourself? Was it for someone important to you? Would you do it all over again?

Take a few deep breaths and let them all out.

Open your eyes.

Now, jot down your notes. You may want to revisit the life vision you wrote in the previous exercise and make a few adjustments.

Notes from Your Guided Meditation

_____

_____

_____

_____

_____

_____

_____

_____

_____

_____

_____

_____

_____

_____

Printable worksheets can be downloaded from
WhereDoIGoFromHere.net

CHAPTER 4

Are Emotional Blocks Hindering Your Success?

Obstacles are those frightful things you see when you take your eyes off your goal.
- Henry Ford

What would hold you back from fulfilling your life vision?

Has it occurred to you that the issues that might prevent you from enjoying success are not inadequate education, lack of experience, insufficient opportunities, the attitudes of your parents and peers, or just plain bad luck? Did you ever think that your obstacles are actually your own feelings and attitudes about yourself?

Have you been working hard for success, but never seem to achieve it? Does it seem like something always stops you before you can accomplish your goals and achieve your personal dreams and aspirations? If so, you're not alone. I see this issue repeatedly. In most cases, people don't feel they *deserve* success, so they never reach it. At some point in their lives, they hobbled themselves with the belief that they were not worthy to enjoy good things in life. Their life vision may be an inspiring idea, but their own emotional roadblocks always keep them at arm's length from their dream.

Our strongest beliefs about ourselves become ingrained at a very early age, usually when we're too young to make reasonable judgments about our surroundings or ourselves.

A small child sees something very bright and shiny. It looks so beautiful, so desirable. The child sets an infantile goal. "Put that bright shiny thing in my mouth." He reaches for it. Suddenly, a parent snatches it away. "No! Bad!" The parent tosses the piece of broken glass into a big can and puts a lid on it. The child internalizes, "My parents will take my goal away from me because I am bad."

An insecure and impressionable pre-teen sits in church and listens to a pastor he has been taught to have complete confidence in. The pastor is preaching about how people who live for the love of money, instead of focusing their life on loving relationships with family and friends will lead empty, unfulfilled lives. The youth internalizes, "I'm not going to make money so I can be liked by everyone."

In both cases, the parent and the pastor are trying to communicate good, positive messages, but the recipient of the messages lacks sufficient understanding and internalizes limiting emotions. It has happened to all of us. Often, those who find their way to success are so brash and self-confident that they have simply learned to ignore negative input and feelings and press ahead. However, there is a more gentle and enjoyable path to success. Change your internal feelings and attitudes so they support you rather than limit you.

Three Steps to Emotional Freedom

Finding freedom from emotional blocks is a lifetime journey. Fortunately, you don't have to complete the journey to start enjoying the benefits; just begin. Today.

Step One: Self-Acceptance

Respect your efforts, respect yourself. Self-respect leads to self-discipline. When you have both firmly under your belt, that's real power.
- Clint Eastwood

The first step on the path to emotional freedom is self-acceptance. To accept yourself is to acknowledge your value and worth just the way you are. That doesn't mean you do not desire or even need to improve. If you want to grow, you need to be able to look squarely at your mistakes, large and small, and say to yourself, "I blew it, but I love and accept myself just the way I am."

Success is not about avoiding mistakes, but about moving past them. If you continue to beat yourself up over past errors in judgment, they will dominate your thoughts and emotions and prevent you from learning and moving on.

Step Two: Forgiveness

Forgiveness is a virtue of the brave.
- Indira Gandhi

Thomas Chalmers, the nineteenth century humanitarian and theologian said, "Unforgiveness is a poison you drink hoping someone else will die." Holding a grudge does no injury to the one with whom you are angry, but it enslaves you emotionally so you cannot move on.

Parents, teachers, and religious leaders all influenced your life in both positive and negative ways. Some of those negative influences helped you form limiting and sometimes self-destructive beliefs, attitudes, and behaviors. It is easy to rationalize that these individuals weren't trying to harm you and therefore don't need forgiveness. Indeed, they may not need forgiveness, but you need to forgive in order to be free from the limiting beliefs created by years of subconscious bitterness. Only after you forgive, can you let go and find freedom.

In some cases, forgiveness seems undeserved. This is often the case in abuse or divorce, but holding onto unforgiveness never hurts those who wronged you. It only hurts you. In fact, unforgiveness gives the one who wronged you a type of control over you. By holding on to unforgiveness, you allow the injury to last a lifetime. Choosing to forgive can cause a chain reaction of healing that will open a doorway to a joyful and fulfilled life.

Jill was raised in a strict religious home. She didn't mind. She truly enjoyed the camaraderie with other young people in her church that gathered around common beliefs and goals. When she went to college, she was introduced to more than she was ready for. But she wanted to fit in so she started drinking at parties, which was followed by recreational drugs and sex. She was attractive and relished her newfound popularity and attention. When she became pregnant, she was unable to tell her parents. She decided to have an abortion. The shame of her decision drove her deep into depression. She considered herself a murderer and hated herself. She left college and returned home, but kept her abortion a secret. Jill moved from one menial job to another. Unconsciously, she gained weight to make herself unattractive to men. She was unable to have a meaningful relationship. Even though she returned to her church and felt forgiven by God, she was unable to forgive herself. Finally, she met with her pastor and told him the whole story. It took time, but she was eventually able to forgive herself. She was then able to rebuild her life, finish college through Internet study, and move on into a successful career. After forgiving and learning to love herself again, she lost the weight she was hiding behind, fell in love, and married. Jill now has two children she loves and cherishes in a special way.

The first person to forgive is yourself. Then, from a place of self-acceptance, you can truly forgive others. Embarrassments and disappointments create deeply rooted resentments. Unfortunately, many people resent themselves. This creates a sense of disqualification.

When you refuse to forgive yourself, you may feel disqualified for a successful, happy life. Crippling shame may arise from something you did, something you failed to do, a belief imposed on you by someone else, a belief you held about others, or simply an emotion you experienced that still haunts you. Whatever is holding you back, it is time to leave your past in the past and move on.

Once you have chosen to love and accept yourself just the way you are, and break the chains of unforgiveness that have held you back, you can begin the journey to become the person you truly want to be.

Step Three: Realize You Deserve to Succeed

Dedicate yourself to the good you deserve and desire for yourself. Give yourself peace of mind. You deserve to be happy. You deserve delight.
- Hannah Arendt

If you grew up in a guilt culture, you may not feel you deserve many good things. Guilt, often injected into our psyche by our parents, teachers, or ministers, can create a strong sense of unworthiness.

I mentioned my East Texas evangelical upbringing before. "I am unworthy" is a mantra of much of Southern evangelicalism. What turned things around for me was a seldom-quoted Bible verse in which Saint Paul writes to one of the churches he founded. He said, "God has made you worthy." [10]

To succeed, we must first change our mantra from "I am unworthy" to "I deserve to be successful." "I deserve to enjoy life." "I AM WORTHY."

"I am worthy because God has made me worthy."

The Key to Your Success

It is never too late to be who you might have been.
- George Eliot

P. T. Barnum had several lackluster businesses. He finally had to declare bankruptcy following his failure as a real estate developer in East Bridgeport, Connecticut at the age of 57. At 61, he went into the circus business with his partner James Anthony Bailey. Together they formed Barnum and Bailey Circus.[11]

Before you can be successful on the outside, you must first become successful on the inside. Success is more about who you are than the size of your bank account. Many famous and wealthy people became rich after years of trying and failing. But their successful nature on the inside kept driving them to succeed financially even after profound failures and setbacks.

Francis Ford Coppola was always a little out of step with the main stream and found himself deeply in debt before his acclaimed release of "*The Godfather*." The income from the movie was not enough, however, and Coppola declared bankruptcy. Although he was a world-renowned film producer, his fortunes were up and down for much of his film career. Late in life, he found his true calling and financial stability as a successful wine entrepreneur.[12]

Walt Disney declared bankruptcy following the failure of his Laugh-O-Gram company.[13] Legend has it he was so poor he went to live in a church basement. To pass the time and sharpen his skill, he sketched the church mice, one of whom he named, Mickey. He later moved to California to become the most successful animator of all time. Mickey went on to become the most famous mouse of all time.

Donald Trump is an aggressive entrepreneur and investor. He, or his companies, have declared bankruptcy four times. But winning more than loosing is the key, and he is currently worth more than $2 billion.[14]

Do you see the pattern? Everyone faces failure. But successful people don't let failure stop them. Solomon, king of Israel, was purported to be the wisest man in the ancient world. In his *Book of Proverbs*, which is found in the *Bible*, he writes, "A good man may fall flat on his face seven times in a row, but he gets up every time."[15] Successful people work their way through failure to ultimate success.

Emotional Blocks Worksheet

The best time to go through this exercise is when you have some time alone and can devote your full attention to it. It will take some soul searching and brutal honesty. When any memory causes an uncomfortable feeling such as guilt, remorse, embarrassment, insecurity, or anger, you'll know the exercise is needed. For some, feelings of superiority or dominance are masks of underlying fears and insecurities. Life is a complex adventure. You may find it necessary to redo the exercise several times regarding the same memory or event, each time uncovering different emotions or beliefs. You'll know the exercise has been successful when the memory no longer causes uncomfortable feelings.

Negative experiences aren't the only ones that can cause unsupportive emotions. Sometimes a positive experience can contribute to an unsupportive belief system. For example, a young person may be praised or even receive a school award for outstanding talent as a writer, artist, or musician. But as life goes on, the individual may become an engineer or businessperson. They may hold feelings of guilt for not living up to the acclaim and expectations of their teachers or peers. Feelings of guilt can hold someone back from being able to devote themselves whole-heartedly to their goals. It can be the same for you, too.

Take several upper and lower breaths before beginning this exercise. It will heighten your awareness and help you get the most from it.

List a time in the past when you felt like a failure due to loss of a job, business venture, relationship, or personal goal.

_____

What was the cause of the failure?

_____

What belief (if any) were you holding at the time that influenced the failure?

_____

In what way did the failure influence your current belief system?

_____

List other persons or events that influenced the failure.

_____

List your own choices that influenced the failure.

_____

_____

Steps to Freedom: Say the following statements aloud, inserting the event that made you feel like a failure. For the forgiveness statement, insert any person or persons you feel were in some way responsible for the failure. Be sure to include yourself. This is a good time to practice an EFT technique discussed later in this chapter. Lightly tap along the front of your collarbone as you repeat the statements. Repeat them until you truly believe them.

Self-Acceptance: "Even though I _list your failure_, I love and accept myself just the way I am."
Forgiveness: "I fully forgive _person's name_ for their contribution to the failure."
Worthiness: "_List the failure_ happened, but I learned from my mistakes and am ready to move on because I'm worthy of success and deserve to succeed."

Printable worksheets can be downloaded from
WhereDoIGoFromHere.net

Why are Beliefs Important?

Myths which are believed in tend to become true.
- George Orwell

Like the ancient Greeks, our lives are shaped by the stories or myths we believe to be true. These include both cultural and personal myths. A cultural myth is something you believe to be true and is believed by everyone or almost everyone within your culture or given sub-culture.

For example, in the nineteenth century the superiority of the "white" race was a nearly universally held belief throughout Europe and North America. This belief was so strongly held that the subjugation of people of color through colonization was considered a noble enterprise. It was epitomized in Rudyard Kipling's poem "_The White Man's Burden._"

Take up the White Man's burden--
Send forth the best ye breed--
Go bind your sons to exile

To serve your captives' need;
To wait in heavy harness,
On fluttered folk and wild--
Your new-caught, sullen peoples,
Half-devil and half-child.[16]

Due to the widespread belief of cultural myths, they are generally supportive of those who live within that group or culture. While the cultural myth of white supremacy was viewed positively by most Europeans as serving their interests, any myth that denies humanity eventually reaps tornadic destruction. Jealousy between European nations over colonial expansion plunged the world into two world wars and devastated the continent for decades.

Personal myths are a different matter. They may be supportive, but not necessarily. Each personal myth or belief about oneself should be examined as to whether or not it supports one's personal goals. We tend to hold on to things we believe to be true because we believe them to be true. The truth is that most things we believe are at least partially true. Few things we believe are absolutely true. I am not saying there are no absolutes. I'm just saying that they are few and far between.

Beliefs Have Consequences

We adopted most of our personal beliefs at a very early age. Generally, someone we trusted told us something we believed rather blindly. Then an event or experience "proved" the belief to us. Consequently, we adopted the belief as one of our personal myths.

Phil had learned from an early age that he was stupid. This belief did not support his goal of getting a graduate degree from an Ivy League school. The issue was that he was dyslexic. He had failed lots of spelling tests. He was also a very slow reader, having to read every word aloud to keep from getting them jumbled up. To be sure, there were elements of truth in his belief. Academics did not come easy for him. Somewhere along the line, Phil realized that having difficulty in school wasn't the same as being stupid. He could choose to hold onto this belief and enjoy a successful career as a plumber. There is nothing wrong with that goal, and a friendly guidance counselor told him it would better suit his talents. But that was not his goal. He believed he had a purpose in life and that purpose called for a graduate degree. His desire for a graduate degree was so great that he was willing to let go of his unsupportive belief. He adopted a new belief that he was not stupid, and he would do whatever it took to succeed at his graduate studies. He had to work twice as hard as anyone else in his class did, but he got his graduate degree from Yale and went on to become a nationally recognized leader in his field.

For children, trusted individuals include parents, older siblings, baby sitters, teachers, and religious community leaders such as scout leaders, rabbis, priests, Sunday school teachers, or ministers.

Beliefs can be either positive or negative, supportive or unsupportive. A positive, supporting belief can be formed when a child hears that they are bright and a good student. They get an A on a test, and the input is confirmed. They form a personal belief about themselves that will likely help them through school. The opposite can also be true. If children hear that they are stupid and then get an F on their first spelling test, they can form a very negative personal belief.

Unfortunately, for many of us, negative input tends to outnumber the positive. That's because we are hardwired to respond quickly and decisively to anything that we perceive as a threat. Parents are generally slow to notice or praise children who are playing quietly. They are quick to respond harshly when the child is running amuck through the house. That's because the child running amuck is in danger of injury or doing damage to the house. The parent's threat instinct kicks in. The poor child doesn't understand that their parents are responding to a threat instinct. They just know they are in trouble again.

People hold onto personal beliefs for a number of reasons, even when they are unsupportive. It may give them a sense of being right. It may give them an excuse to be lazy and not even try. The real question is, "Does this belief support my personal goals?" If not, leave the belief behind and go for your goal.

Our beliefs shape our attitudes. Our attitudes result in our actions. Our actions form our habits. Our habits determine how successful we will be in all of life's endeavors including our job, relationships, hobbies, and spiritual expression.

Money, Oh Money, Oh Where Did You Go?

I've met people who have never earned over $100,000 a year and yet are millionaires. I have met more people who earn $250,000 a year or more and have a net worth of zero. What's the difference?

You can point to obvious issues such as money management, but the true issue is the individual's belief about themselves. People are poor money managers because they spend more than they make. People overspend because of a poor sense of self-worth.

A poor sense of self-worth can take several financial avenues.

Un-Deserver: People feel they are unworthy to have money, so they spend it to get rid of it. They may spend their money on charities or lavish gifts for others. They may just blow it all on expensive trips and hobbies.

Approval Seeker: These people spend what they feel they need to in order to fit in with a certain group. They may spend their money on big houses, fancy cars, or other things to impress their friends or to feel as successful as their neighbors.

Self-Destructor: People inwardly hate themselves so they subconsciously injure themselves by spending money, often on gambling or high-risk investments.

Most people I work with have some jagged edges to their self-image. I have met very few perfectly balanced people. Many people have some tendencies toward self-abasement or even self-destruction. In extreme cases, professional help is needed.

If you have picked up some unsupporting self-concepts along your life-journey, here are simple steps you can take to improve your sense of self.
1. Identify the beliefs that are holding you back.
2. Identify and deal with the source of those beliefs.
3. Create new beliefs that will support your pursuit of success.

The following worksheet will help you identify and deal with unsupportive personal beliefs.

Changing Unsupportive Beliefs Worksheet

What unsupportive belief am I holding onto that's keeping me from personal success?

_____

What happened that caused me to adopt this belief?

_____

What event, experience, or feeling confirmed this belief?

_____

What do I gain from holding this belief?

_____

Does this belief support my personal aspirations and goals?

_____

If not, why not?

_____

What is true about this belief?

_____

What is false about this belief?

_____

If I continue to hold this belief without question, what will happen to me?

_____

How has holding onto this belief contributed to my being where I am today?

_____

How has holding onto this belief affected the people I love?

_____

What new belief would better support my personal goals?

_____

Printable worksheets can be downloaded from
WhereDoIGoFromHere.net

Professional Resources

Often we have blind spots that hide the emotional blocks to our success. Having a professional coach or consultant can be very helpful. There are also several do-it-yourself techniques you can apply.

98

Traditional vs. Non-Traditional Therapy

A licensed, trained psychologist, counselor, or therapist can be a great ally in your quest for emotional freedom. Your family physician or other trusted medical professional can provide a referral. In addition, your priest, rabbi or other religious leader may be able to refer you to resources that can sometimes be available at a reduced rate.

Emotional Freedom Technique (EFT)

Gary Craig developed EFT, which involves the activation of meridian points to raise your energy level and stimulate emotional release as you work your way through issues that are preventing optimum performance. No needles are used. You stimulate the meridian points by tapping with your fingertips.

There are dozens of meridian points used by EFT practitioners. There are several meridians along the collarbone. So, for simplicity, I suggest beginners just tap along the front of the collarbone to begin to experience some of the benefits of EFT. This is an especially helpful practice when going through the Emotional Blocks Worksheet.

From Gary Craig's website (emofree.com) you can learn more about the technique, download a free EFT Manual, view demonstrations, and learn how to locate local practitioners.

Hypnosis

Hypnosis can help you remember and deal with events that were so traumatic that you have blocked their memory. Often sexual abuse by a trusted family member can be a blocked memory. Even though the memory is blocked, the emotion surrounding the event will haunt you your entire life and prevent you from enjoying optimum success. In most cases, there is nothing as dramatic as sexual abuse or suppressed memories to uncover. Typically, simple events that were misunderstood during early childhood because of your inexperience can be hidden. Those events are often forgotten, not because of trauma, but because at some point we discarded them as "silly." The emotion however, still lingers. Your coach can help you find a reputable hypnotherapist in your area.

Professional Consulting and Coaching

Not long ago, professional coaching was limited to very few professions where high competition demanded top performance to succeed. Athletes, actors, and opera singers all employed coaches, but very few business people considered hiring a coach necessary for their success. Times have changed. Today, professional consultants and coaches exist for people in every field of endeavor. Many specialize in areas such as job search, entrepreneurship, sales, or corporate management. Others offer services that are more general and market themselves as personal or life coaches.

My own consulting and coaching service offers a "faith-based" approach. By "faith-based," I don't mean that I endorse a particular faith system such as Christian Evangelicalism or Zen Buddhism. I simply start with the premise that there is a spiritual dimension to life that cannot be ignored. I will talk more about the three-faith model in Chapter 10.

An important aspect of my own consulting and coaching is the practice of intentional breathing and *Stillness*. You can live for weeks without food. You can live for days without water. You can only survive a few minutes without breath. This most essential element in our lives is also the most powerful. With the proper application of intentional breathing, you can discover new ideas, heal yourself of old emotional wounds, and create a new you.

Guided Meditation:
Created to Succeed

A CD of this meditation is available from Amazon.com and other retail outlets.

Find a place where you will not be observed or disturbed.

Sit up straight in a comfortable position.

Close your eyes.

Allow yourself to breathe naturally. Take breath in. Let breath out.

Now take a deep cleansing breath in through your nose, if possible. Notice the rise and fall of your chest and abdomen. Notice the sense of chill as the cool air passes through your nostrils. Blow it all out, pushing up with your diaphragm to empty your lungs completely. Take a second cleansing breath to rejuvenate your lungs with fresh air.

Take a few upper breaths, focusing on pushing the air into the chest portion of your lungs. Take your fingertips and touch your heart. Feel your chest move up and down as you take each breath. Breathe in, through your nose if possible, and out through your mouth. If you can't breathe that way, don't worry. That technique is just a way to help take your mind off other things and concentrate on your breath.

Now take a few lower breaths, focusing on pushing air as deeply into your abdomen as possible. Again, breathe in, through your nose if possible, and out through your mouth. As you inhale, imagine yourself breathing in positive

energy. As you exhale, imagine yourself breathing out
negative energy. Say to yourself:

> *Breathe in peace; breathe out anxiety.*
> *Breathe in faith; breathe out doubt.*
> *Breathe in love; breathe out indifference.*
> *Breathe in hope; breathe out despair.*
> *Breathe in confidence; breathe out timidity.*

Empty your mind of feelings of stress or anxiety. Thoughts
about problems at work or home may rush in at this point.
That's normal. Don't fight the thoughts. Just acknowledge
them and let them slip away.

Relax your body. Focus on your head. Recognize any
tension in your scalp, face, or jaw. Will each area to relax.
Let your jaw slip down slightly into a relaxed position.
Now focus on your neck and shoulders. Again, recognize
any tension and will each area to relax. Repeat this
relaxation technique for your arms and chest. As you focus
on your diaphragm, your breathing may alter a bit. You
may begin to breathe a little more deeply and regularly as if
asleep. Continue the technique, moving down your body
until you reach your toes. Take a moment to realize that
you are fully relaxed.

In your mind's eye, picture yourself walking down a forest
trail. All around you is green. The earth is soft beneath your
feet. The overhead canopy casts a greenish glow all around
you.

You walk out of the trail onto a beach, warm sand beneath
your feet. A large body of water is before you, but it is
unlike any other lake, river, or ocean you have ever seen. It
is so big and vast that you cannot see the other side. And
the water is crystal clear, like a spring-fed pool. You see no

rocks, only white sand leading gently down into the water. You hear the gentle lapping of waves. You hear a bird chirping. The air smells clean. You expect to smell salt, as if you were at the ocean. But instead, all you smell is a fresh cleanness, as if this water cleanses all it touches, even the air that passes above it.

Bright sunlight engulfs you. You feel the warmth of the sun on your face. Since you're all alone, you strip off your clothing until you're naked, feeling the sun warm your skin.

You slowly walk into the water. You find the water refreshingly cool. You feel the sand and water surround your feet and notice even more tension drain away from you. As you walk deeper, the water's refreshing coolness engulfs your thighs and hips. You have a sensation of being cleansed as the water rises to your stomach and chest. As it reaches your shoulders, you lean back and float effortlessly.

You relax and breathe easily, deeply, and naturally. With your ears beneath the surface of the water, the water engulfs you in silence. In that complete silence you hear a gentle voice speaking to you softly. You recognize it as the voice of God. You recognize it because you knew that voice as a young child, before worries and fears and the noise of other's expectations drowned it out. The voice of God speaks three things to you.

"I love you."

"I created you to succeed and prosper."

"I created you to enjoy my goodness."

As you float effortlessly in this cleansing pool, you meditate on what those three words mean in your relationship with your family and friends.

"I love you."

"I created you to succeed and prosper."

"I created you to enjoy my goodness."

As you relax in complete peace, you reflect on what those three words mean in your vocation, job, or business.

"I love you."

"I created you to succeed and prosper."

"I created you to enjoy my goodness."

As all pain and disappointment of your past are washed away by the purity of this pond, you visualize what those three words mean for your future.

"I love you."

"I created you to succeed and prosper."

"I created you to enjoy my goodness."

It is time to leave the water. You stand up and feel the soft sand beneath your feet. As you walk back to the beach, you feel the water drain away from your body. Beginning with your head and shoulders, then draining from your chest, stomach, hips, legs, and feet. As the water drains from your body, you feel renewed as if all fear and self-doubt are being removed from you, washed away by the pure spring.

You stand again on the beach, warmed by the sun. You feel refreshed. You are empowered with a new life and vision. You are filled with a new strength. You are ready to step back into the activities of your daily life, but with renewed hope and joy.

Notes from Your Guided Meditation

CHAPTER 5

Can Affirmations Create a Success Oriented Mindset?

The question isn't who is going to let me; it's who is going to stop me.
- Ayn Rand in <u>The Fountainhead</u>

A do-it-yourselfer is tacking up some molding for his room remodel. His hammer misses the nail and slams into his thumb. "You idiot!" He exclaims, "When are you going to learn to use a hammer?" Across town, another do-it-yourselfer meets his thumb with a hammer. "That's not like you," he tells himself. "You're usually more careful than that." Both would-be carpenters are creating internal expectations about their future skill. The second will likely improve. The first will likely stay the same.

What you say to yourself about yourself is an affirmation that will have an impact on who you will become. In fact, your affirmations made you what you are today. Other people may praise you or condemn you, but it is what you say about yourself that matters.

Sheila was a moderately successful psychologist. She had a good job and made enough money to live on. However, like the majority of Americans, she lived month to month. She became frustrated with always being caught up, but never getting ahead. A friend challenged her to discover the limiting belief that was keeping her from true financial success. Sheila protested that she didn't have any limiting beliefs. Still, she devoted time to go through an exercise designed to uncover any limiting beliefs. She repeated the exercise four times before it dawned on her: She had a long-standing, firmly held belief that it was wrong to want more than enough money to get by. Her goals had always revolved around having enough. Enough to pay the bills. Enough to buy food and clothing. A nice enough house to live in. From somewhere in her past, she acquired the belief that she didn't deserve more than just enough to get by. She used affirmations to help change her beliefs about herself. She repeated to herself, "I do deserve it." "I am worth it." "I can have it." When an investment opportunity came her way, she balked at first. It seemed unwise to take a risk. Then, she realized that she was just falling back into her old limiting belief system. Her underlying feelings of being unworthy of financial success were masquerading as wise caution. After proper research, she decided the investment was a sound one. It led to profits, increased investments, and finally real wealth. Sheila is no longer limited by having enough to get by. She can enjoy expensive vacations, a nice wardrobe, and a wonderful lifestyle because she deserves it. However, first, she had to believe she deserved it.

Think about how you became the way you are – both good and bad. Someone believed in you and told you that you would do great in business. You believed them and often repeated to yourself, "I am going to do great in business." You then went on and did well in business. Or maybe you didn't believe them. You said to yourself, "I've sure got them fooled. I don't know anything about business." My guess is that you have experienced less success than you could have.

Perhaps someone didn't believe in you. You heard. "You'll never amount to anything." If you agreed with them and said to yourself, "They're right. I will never accomplish anything of value," then you're probably living an unsatisfying life, frustrated because you know you could do more and can't figure out why you seem stuck below your potential. But if you said to yourself, "I'll show them. I'll make something great of myself," then you're probably enjoying success in your chosen field of endeavor.

In each example, what matters is not what others have told you about yourself, but what you believed and told yourself about yourself. In other words, you have created who you are by the unconscious application of the affirmation process. You have either affirmed your *self* into success, or affirmed your *self* into an average or below average existence.

The good news is that once you realize that you are the product of your own self talk and beliefs about yourself, you can change yourself from who you are now into who you want to be by employing the same method. We discussed changing unsupportive beliefs in the previous chapter. Now let's deal with the issue of self talk.

Everyone talks to himself or herself. Sometimes these conversations are out loud, but usually they're so quiet you may not even hear yourself speaking. The conversation originates in your subconscious mind, which has developed a system of beliefs about you. These are beliefs either you or someone else put there, and you accepted as fact. Once those beliefs are firmly established, your subconscious continuously measures your thoughts, actions, words, and ideas against your belief about yourself.

Too many of us never even try to enjoy real success in our lives because of negative, limiting beliefs. Here are some

examples of supportive and non-supportive self talk. Each
affirms something positive or negative about us.

Supportive	Non-Supportive
I am worthy to enjoy good things in life.	I don't deserve that raise.
I can learn the new application and be very proficient at it.	It's too hard. I'll never get it.
Mistakes are a part of life. I learn from them and keep going.	I can't believe I did something so stupid. I should just quit now.
I enjoy doing whatever it takes to have the best relationship possible with my spouse.	Most marriages end in divorce, so it's going to end eventually. Why bother trying?
I enjoy getting to work 30 minutes early so I can start my day sharp, prepared and on my game.	Work is drudgery. I think I should just sleep in. No one will care if I'm a few minutes late.
I am thrilled to do my best at whatever endeavor I pursue.	If it wasn't good enough, they wouldn't call it the minimum.

I think you get the idea. It may sound like you're talking to
yourself in "bumper sticker" at first, but here's the thing:
Supportive affirmations move you closer to your goal; non-
supportive affirmations move you farther from your goal.
Which direction do you want to go?

***You must see yourself as a success BEFORE you become
successful, not after.***

You will never succeed in anything without changing your
non-supportive beliefs into supportive beliefs. New self talk

in the form of supportive affirmations is an important tool in accomplishing your goals.

One important thing to remember here is that self talk without belief and visualization is worthless. Every day you may read aloud an affirmation that you are confident and brave, but if inwardly you're saying to yourself, "Who am I kidding?" the affirmation will have no effect. It is imperative that you believe the affirmation, or at least believe you can acquire, achieve, or become the goal expressed in the affirmation.

It's also important that your affirmation creates an image that can be grasped by your inner self. As I mentioned earlier, your subconscious doesn't think in words as your conscious mind does. Rather, it processes thoughts in symbols and images. This is where many people fail to reap the potential benefits of the affirmation process. They think that if they write good affirmations, then they should come true. Without an accompanying image, though, an affirmation is just a conscious mental exercise with little benefit.

When I first started my consulting business, I worked primarily with individuals pursuing business startups. As such, I worked with many people who opened their own businesses. Many factors predict success or failure. These factors are keys that unlock success for an individual. The first key to unlock success is believing you deserve success. If you do not believe you deserve it, you will never allow yourself to have it.

There is no better time than now to take conscious control of your affirmation process and affirm your *self* into the ideal you. We will talk about how to craft the best affirmations for you later in this chapter.

Avoid a Presumptuous Attitude

A positive attitude about yourself is a powerful thing. But little can be more destructive than a presumptuous attitude about the future.

Positive, self-confidence: "I choose my actions wisely, for they have the power to make my dreams possible."[17] Presumption: "Everything will get better because I want it to."

A positive attitude will make you into a stronger person. It will encourage you to work hard. It will remind you to be patient and use your resources wisely. A presumptuous attitude will make you lazy and expect others to do your work for you. It will encourage you to be in a hurry, waste your resources, fall for get-rich-quick schemes, and spend your money before the harvest.

In a research study conducted jointly by New York University and the University of Hamburg, positive fantasies about the future resulted in poor decision-making, stress, and lowered energy levels.[18]

There is a difference between being caught up in pie-in-the-sky fantasies and embracing a positive attitude about yourself and your abilities. A positive attitude moves your life forward. A presumptuous attitude just leaves you confused as to why your life is spiraling downward, out of control.

Become the Ideal You

The will to win, the desire to succeed, the urge to reach your full potential...these are the keys that will unlock the door to personal excellence.
- Confucius

What would you change about yourself to make you a happier, healthier, more successful person? Would you read more? Exercise more? Would you be more self-motivated? More assertive? More patient? More understanding? More open? More demanding? Would you delegate more, or less? Would you complain less? Work harder? Be more responsive to your family?

Three things to remember:
All you can improve is yourself.
Your only starting place is here.
The only time you have is now.

Think about the ideal *you*. What does the ideal *you* look like? What does the ideal *you* say? How does the ideal *you* act in a given circumstance? Where does the ideal *you* work? What does the ideal *you* do in leisure? Hold that image in front of yourself daily. You can become who you want to be.

Write a description of yourself the way you want to be. Do you want to be intellectual, outgoing, courageous, confident, kind, generous...? You make the list. Take some time to think it through. What habits do you want to have? Do you want to exercise daily? Pray? Meditate? Write it out in detail.

Qualities and Attributes

List five to ten qualities or attributes the ideal you would possess. Include anything you believe would contribute to your ultimate success.

1. _____

2. _____

3. _____

4. _____

5. _____

6. _____

7. _____

8. _____

9. _____

10. _____

Printable worksheets can be downloaded from WhereDoIGoFromHere.net

Once you know who you want to be, create affirmations that reinforce the attributes of the ideal you.

Each attribute-related affirmation should
1. Start with "I am."
2. State the quality or attitude you want to be a part of the new ideal "you."

3. Have a statement that expands, clarifies, or
    exemplifies your new quality or attitude.
4. Be specific about the description of the new you.

Here are some examples.

*I am confident. I am confident in myself, in my ideas, and in
my abilities. I am confident in those who support me,
especially my wife, family, friends, and business associates.*

*I am creative. I have great ideas and pursue them
confidently and vigorously.*

*I am resilient. I don't panic at problems or complain about
setbacks. I know that every adversity can be overcome with
faith, patience, endurance, creativity, and hard work. Every
adversity I overcome makes me stronger.*

Write an affirmation for each of your ideal qualities or
attributes.

1. _____

_____

_____

2. _____

_____

_____

3. _____

_____

116

4. _____

_____

_____

5. _____

_____

_____

Printable worksheets can be downloaded from
WhereDoIGoFromHere.net

Habits

List five to ten daily habits that you would like to be part of the ideal you.

1. _____

2. _____

3. _____

4. _____

5. _____

6. _____

7. _____

8. _____

9. _____

10. _____

Once you know who you want to be, create affirmations that reinforce the ideal you.

Each habit-related affirmation should
1. Start with "I am."
2. Include an emotionally charged adverb.
3. Include a strong verb.
4. Be specific about the description of the new you.

Here are some examples.

I am enthusiastically meeting new clients wherever I go.

I am joyously playing with my children for an hour at least three times a week.

I am happily studying 30 minutes each evening for my certification exam.

Write an affirmation for each of your ideal habits.

1. _____

_____

2. _____

_____

3. _____

118

4. _____

5. _____

Read your affirmations aloud at least twice each day. Say them first thing in the morning and last thing at night.

Emotionally Charged Affirmations

All we need to do is remember a particularly embarrassing moment, and we will have the same physical sensations associated with the situation. Our stomach will turn upside down. Our blood pressure will rise. We may consciously or unconsciously avoid similar situations associated with the embarrassment. Many young teens have an awkward moment with a member of the opposite sex while they are trying to figure things out. Those youthful embarrassments can have long-term repercussions, even to the point of spending the rest of their lives avoiding the opposite sex. We tend to repeat behavior that has given us a sense of security in the past and avoid behavior that has left us feeling uncertain and awkward. This can be caused by something as simple as having a boy or girl you liked laugh at you, or as serious as emotional or physical abuse from someone you trusted. Generally, the more serious the causal event, the more profound the behavioral result. Emotions are powerful links to memories, and our memories are powerful links to our actions. The important thing to remember is that any stored emotional memory can have a lasting effect unless it is dealt with, as we discussed earlier.

Naturally, emotional memories can be positive, as well. Scoring the winning touchdown. Being voted class president. Receiving recognition from your friends or peers. Having your childhood sweetheart take your hand and give you that coveted first kiss. These all create positive emotional memories. Remember what it felt like when you won a competition, gave birth to your children, made your first sale, or received your first promotion.

It is the power of positive emotions that you want to draw on when you say your affirmations. Take a moment to reflect on a few of those events that were energized with positive emotions before you start reciting your affirmations. That excitement will act to supercharge your affirmations and increase their effectiveness.

Visualize Your Affirmations

Visualize this thing that you want, see it, feel it, believe in it. Make your mental blue print, and begin to build.
- Robert Collier

Attach your affirmation to a meaningful, related image. "See" yourself as fulfilling your affirmations.

If you have an exercise-related affirmation such as, "I am diligently exercising each day to keep in shape and maintain my ideal body weight," then visualize yourself enjoying your favorite exercise. I use pictures with my affirmations to help me visualize their fulfillment. Since I often say my affirmations while at the computer, I created a slide show presentation that flashes my affirmation statements with pictures that display iconic images. For example, one of my affirmations is "I am a business man of integrity, deservedly trusted by my friends and clients." The image that goes with that affirmation is a picture of a lighthouse, boldly shining its light over a storm-tossed sea. That image speaks integrity to me. It reinforces the affirmation and gives it a visual emphasis. You can also visualize yourself in a situation that calls for integrity and "see" yourself fulfilling your ideal self-image.

Take time to review the images you choose so they truly reinforce your affirmations because of their meaning to you. If you like, you can use subliminal software to flash images on your computer periodically. You may not even notice the images appearing, but your subconscious will absorb their impact. You can print the images and hang them in a prominent place in your office so you see them often. Or, put them in a photo album and browse through them from time to time. All of these methods will reinforce the creation of the new ideal "you."

Breathe Your Affirmations

We discussed deep breathing exercises in the introductory chapter on the practice of *Stillness*. Deep breathing pumps extra oxygen to your brain. Oxygenation of your brain enhances sensory awareness and helps you think more clearly. When used in conjunction with your affirmations, it helps your affirmations take hold with greater strength. Intentional breathing can actually improve creation of new neuro-pathways so that deeply rooted habits change more quickly.

Changing old habits that don't support your life goals into new habits that do support your life goals is no easy task. Deep breathing exercises are a great tool to help enact that change.

Strengthen Your Affirmations Through Meditation

When you are in a meditative state, your conscious mind can receive inspiration and insight from your intuitive inner self. Also, your subconscious is open to new input from your conscious mind. It's like opening a doorway between your conscious and subconscious mind. That's why affirmations used in conjunction with meditation or the practice of *Stillness* can change you from the inside out.

Jesus told a story about a widow who was wronged by a wealthy man who was politically powerful in his local community. The widow went to the local judge for redress, but the judge was not a good man. He refused to help her because of her opponent's position. Still, the widow hounded the judge day and night until the judge finally relented and forced the powerful man to return to her what he had taken.[19]

When you're trying to change long-standing, non-supportive attitudes or habits, be like the persistent widow. Keep hounding your inner self until you're fully transformed and have effortlessly adopted new attitudes and habits that support and sustain you.

Guided Meditation:
Using Affirmations

A CD of this meditation is available from Amazon.com and other retail outlets.

Here is a simple way to use the practice of *Stillness* to allow your affirmations to take root in your subconscious mind in a very powerful way. The power of relaxation and focus in the meditation increase the energy of your affirmations.

If you want to go through all of your affirmations, you will need to set aside about 30 minutes for the exercise. However, you can choose two or three critical affirmations and perform the exercise in 5-10 minutes. It is very powerful to focus selected affirmations at bedtime. By reviewing a few of your most pressing affirmations just before you go to sleep, your subconscious can work on the affirmations throughout the night.

Find a place where you will not be observed or disturbed.

Sit up straight in a comfortable position.

Close your eyes.

Allow yourself to breathe naturally. Take breath in. Let breath out.

Now take a deep cleansing breath in through your nose, if possible. Notice the rise and fall of your chest and abdomen. Notice the sense of chill as the cool air passes through your nostrils. Blow it all out, pushing up with your diaphragm to empty your lungs completely. Take a second cleansing breath to rejuvenate your lungs with fresh air.

Take a few upper breaths, focusing on pushing the air into the chest portion of your lungs. Take your fingertips and touch your heart. Feel your chest move up and down as you take each breath. Breathe in, through your nose if possible, and out through your mouth. If you can't breathe that way, don't worry. That technique is just a way to help take your mind off other things and concentrate on your breath.

Now take a few lower breaths, focusing on pushing air as deeply into your abdomen as possible. Again, breathe in, through your nose if possible, and out through your mouth. As you inhale, imagine yourself breathing in positive energy. As you exhale, imagine yourself breathing out negative energy. Say to yourself:

Breathe in peace; breathe out anxiety.
Breathe in faith; breathe out doubt.
Breathe in love; breathe out indifference.
Breathe in hope; breathe out despair.
Breathe in confidence; breathe out timidity.

Empty your mind of stress and anxiety. Thoughts about problems at work or home may rush in at this point. That's normal. Don't fight the thoughts. Just acknowledge them and let them slip away.

Relax your body. Focus on your head. Recognize any tension in your scalp, face, or jaw. Will each area to relax. Let your jaw slip down slightly into a relaxed position. Now focus on your neck and shoulders, letting your shoulders drop slightly. Again, recognize any tension and will each area to relax. Repeat this relaxation technique for your arms and chest. As you focus on your diaphragm, your breathing may alter a bit. You may begin to breathe a little more deeply and regularly as if asleep. Continue the technique, moving down your body until you reach your toes. Take a moment to realize that you are fully relaxed.

In your mind's eye, imagine a door. Open the door and see a stairway leading down into a room filled with love and peace. The love and peace are thick and tangible as if they were some kind of liquid filling the space. Enter the room and close the door behind you. You're all alone. No one is there to observe you. You are free to be your true self. Slowly descend the stairway into the room filled with love and peace. With each step, you feel yourself more absorbed into the love and peace of the room. Imagine the love and peace consuming your body. First your feet. Then your ankles. Slowly you descend the stairs. Slowly your body is consumed by love and peace. Your knees are now consumed by love and peace. Your midsection is now consumed by love and peace. Your stomach, your heart, and your chest are now consumed by love and peace. Continue down the stairs. Finally, your head and your brain are now consumed by love and peace. Take a moment to experience the most incredible, peaceful existence you have ever experienced. You feel weightless, as if floating in an ocean. The physical sensations of your body seem to have drifted away. There is no judgment here. Grudges cannot be held here. Anger and resentments have all floated away in this ocean of love, joy, and peace. Only positive energy exists here. You can only have positive thoughts and feelings about yourself and about everyone else.

In this beautiful place, say your first affirmation. Feel its wonderful power. Believe it is true. Imagine how your life has just changed. Repeat the affirmation. Savor its reality. Say it a third time. Know that it is yours and no one can take it away. Now move to your second affirmation. Speak

it slowly three times. Again, feel its power. Know it is real.
Know it is yours. Continue slowly through each
affirmation. There is no need to rush because there is no
time here.

Once you have gone through all the affirmations you
intended, imagine yourself turning around 180 degrees.
When you turn around you discover a mirror. In the mirror,
you see the new you. This is similar to the ideal you that
you wrote about in an earlier exercise, only better, more
pure than you could have possibly imagined. Walk toward
the mirror until you actually walk into the mirror, melding
yourself and the image of the new you into one. Feel the
power of the new you fill your being. Take a moment to
relish this transformation. You may smile, laugh, or cry.
Anything is okay. There is no judgment here.

Soon you will feel a release and know it is time to return.
You see the stairs again. Walk toward them and slowly
begin to ascend. With each step, you feel the physical
sensations of your body return. You may need to pause on
the stairs as you feel your weight and the tug of gravity
again. You're not sad, though, because you will always
hold the memory of this place in your mind and its glow in
your heart.

When you reach the door, open it and step back into the
conscious world. Open your eyes and see your
surroundings. Tell yourself, "*I am not sad because I hold
the memory of that place in my mind and its glow in my
heart.*"

Notes from Your Guided Meditation

_____

_____

_____

_____

_____

_____

_____

_____

_____

_____

_____

Printable worksheets can be downloaded from
WhereDoIGoFromHere.net

BOOK TWO

CREATE YOUR SUCCESS

CHAPTER 6

Allocate Resources to Your Goal

Don't judge each day by the harvest you reap but by the seeds that you plant.
- Robert Louis Stevenson

Jesus told a story about a tiny mustard seed that grew into a tree large enough to provide shelter to the birds of the air.[20] Do you have a seed you would like to plant and watch miraculously grow into something that far exceeded your imagination?

Perhaps you are a parent whose goal is to plant seeds of integrity, faith, and enterprise in your children.

Perhaps your goal is to bring joy and inspiration to those around you through music, writing, dance, or visual arts.

Perhaps your goal is to plant a business that grows large enough to provide sustenance to hundreds or thousands of employees. Remember, accomplishing your goal isn't just about you. In fact, if the only reason you want to build a business is to provide income for yourself, you will probably fail. You would be better off getting a job. But if your reason to open a business is to care for your community, your customers, and your employees, genuine success is virtually guaranteed.

Perhaps your goal is not a business, but an altruistic organization that provides much-needed assistance to others.

Perhaps your goal is even more personal, such as looking for the development of a long term-intimate relationship.

Whatever your ultimate goal, you must first plant some seeds before it can grow into reality.

Planting Your Seeds

Plant the seeds of failure, and failure will be expressed; plant the seeds of success, and success is assured.
- Dr. Forrest C. Shaklee, Sr.

Everyone has seeds to sow. Sow the seeds that will bring the harvest you desire.

Zig Ziglar, the famous motivational speaker, told the following story often.

Dave Anderson was a crew foreman for the railroad. He had enjoyed an average career working his way up on the rail crew until he made it to the highest level he had dreamed possible, crew foreman. One day while he and his crew were working on a bad patch of track, a passenger car pulled onto the side rail. Jim Murphy stuck his head out of the window and shouted, "Hey Dave, is that you? Come on over and visit a spell." Dave and Jim visited over lunch in his private railroad car, catching up with each other and reminiscing over old times. When Dave returned to his crew, the men were dumbstruck. "How did you come to be friends with the president of the railroad?" they asked. Dave responded, "Jim and I began working here on the same day and on the same crew. The difference is that I went to work for $1.75 an hour. Jim went to work for the railroad."

If you're looking for improved financial status, sow seeds that relate to your finances. You may not have financial resources to give to a worthy cause. But donating two hours a month to a homeless shelter or donating food to a local charity can go a long way to release abundance into your life.

If you're looking for improved relationships, sow seeds into your relationships or prospective relationships. Offer a smile to the people you work with. Give a listening ear to someone you know. Visit someone who is lonely.

If you're looking for a job, consider volunteering somewhere during your job search. Many people have networked their way into a great job through their volunteer network. Others have been offered jobs by the very organization they were volunteering for. Be careful that your motive is not exclusively to volunteer so you can create a network or find a job. The motive is to volunteer so you can give. Jesus said, "Give to others, and it will be given back to you, in the greatest abundance possible." [21]

If you're looking for improvement in your job, give your greatest effort at work and a genuine interest in the future of your company.

Whatever your goal, accomplishing it will require seeds of both time and investment.

The Time-Money Equation

Time is money.
- Benjamin Franklin

Building a successful future requires the investment of two key resources, time, and money. In business, these resources are interchangeable, at least to some extent. If you have very little time to invest in an enterprise, you can compensate for your lack of time by investing more money in the enterprise. You can hire a manager, employ some marketers, and bring in consultants to develop systems and processes that put your new business venture on automatic pilot.

If you have very little money to invest in your new enterprise, you can compensate for your lack of investment capital by investing more time in getting it off the ground. You can do your own marketing, develop your own systems, and work 80 hours a week running your business by yourself.

I often work with clients who want a semi-absentee business that pays them $100,000 a year with a $20,000 investment. I tell them, "You can build a business over several years by devoting a great deal of time and energy, or you can invest $500,000 and start a semi-absentee business that can pay you $100,000 the first year."

Before committing to a business venture, take a realistic inventory of yourself. How much money and time do you have to invest in the new venture? Will it be sufficient? Often we tell ourselves, "This idea will work as long as...." We look to luck to make up for our lack of resources. Instead, ask yourself, "Do I have sufficient time and money to invest in my new business to make it work in a worst-case scenario?" If not, you may want to scale down your plans. Ensuring a small success upon which you can build larger successes, is a better strategy than going for the brass ring when you have insufficient resources to weather a storm or two along the way.

In other endeavors, there is no substitute for time and personal effort. There is a saying in athletics, "You can't hire someone else to do your pushups for you." We all cheer Olympians as they mount the awards platform, not just for their victory, but also for their years of dedication and hard work that got them there. We applaud the soloist in the orchestra, knowing that their fifteen seconds of perfection is the culmination of years of study and practice. In developing personal relationships, there is no substitute for time. The concept that small amounts of quality time are as good as large quantities of average time is a fallacy. Quality time is important, but what people who count on you want most is to know that you are there for them.

Your Money Seed

Anyone can start where they are. I know a very successful businessperson who built a strong retail business that's a hub of his local community. He began his new business venture selling tires out of his pickup truck on the side of the highway. His retail outlet now grosses over $1.5 million a year. The early years were rough, but he started with what he had and built from there.

Make a realistic assessment of how much you can invest. If you have a lot of capital, don't rush to spend it. Starting too big or growing too fast are killers for new businesses. If you have very little, prepare for your new business by saving the money you will need. Determine a set percentage of your paycheck to set aside each month to raise startup capital for your business. When you're ready, start where you are and grow slowly.

Luciano, Carlo, Gilberto, and Giuliana were four siblings who liked colorful clothing. They made sweaters for themselves, which were admired and desired. To satisfy the requests from friends and family they made sweaters on their kitchen table using a borrowed knitting machine. As demand grew, Luciano sold his bicycle to purchase the machine. Today the Benetton family grosses over $3 billion dollars in sales annually.[23]

And then there's Steve Jobs: He started Apple Computer in his garage. It's okay to start small.

Your Time Seed

Kim discovered that she really enjoyed resting her head on a warm pillow. It seemed to dissipate the tension of the day and helped her relax. She enjoyed it so much that she made a few to give as gifts to her children's teachers. After putting up with those kids all day, she figured they would enjoy the pillow as much as she did. She filled the pillow with small corn kernels that could be warmed in a microwave. When her husband lost his job, she thought that she might be able to help with the household income by making her microwavable pillows and selling a few. She sold them from the back of her truck. That was so successful, she moved to a mall kiosk. Now her pillows sell in major department stores and generate over $1 million in sales each year.[22]

A great many people start side businesses while they have full-time jobs. The strength of this strategy is that you don't need to take a salary from your new business while it grows and builds a strong capital position. The weakness of this strategy is that it can be difficult to do a good job at your place of employment while building your new business. If you are attempting this, the key to success is to start small.

Any venture requires the seed of time. Developing skill takes time. Building relationships takes time. Creating your success takes time. You will devote time to your business, your relationships, even your hobbies if you want to be successful at them.

Many successful entrepreneurs will tell you that they spent 70-80 hours a week launching their first business until it achieved profitability, a process that usually takes about three years. There's nothing wrong with that approach, as long as you know what you're in for.

You can make more money. You can gain more knowledge. But you cannot create more time. Plant your time seeds carefully and wisely.

Make Time Work for You

This is the key to time management - to see the value of every moment. So during those first moments of the day, which are yours and yours alone, you can circumvent these boundaries and concentrate fully on spiritual matters. And this gives you the opportunity to plan the time management of the entire day.
- Menachem Mendel Schneerson

Contrary to popular opinion, 24 hours really are enough time in a day to get done what truly needs to be done. If you prioritize your tasks, plan your day, and follow your plan, your accomplishments will be amazing.

Time management is really all about choice. Many people get in trouble by allowing external forces to make their choices for them. Your boss, your spouse, your kids, your neighbors, and your relatives may want to disagree, but you are the one who is in control of your life and your time. Many people let others dictate how they spend their time.

However, if you choose that path, be prepared to accomplish very little, if anything at all.

Make the choices that will make your life productive and successful.

Choices

Live as if you were already living for the second time and as if you had acted the first time as wrongly as you are about to act now.
- Victor Frankel

Your choices determine your future.

Your freedom of choice is one of your greatest super-powers. It also comes with great responsibility.

Once you make your choice, only you can stop you.

The only way to fail is to quit.

Know where you are going, and keep moving in that direction. Whatever you do, don't stop. Things outside of your control may slow you down, but stopping is your choice alone.

Choose to keep moving forward. Your ultimate success may not look like what you envisioned in the beginning, but succeed you will.

Life doesn't just happen; it unfolds through a succession of choices.

Choices produce action. Consistent action produces habits.

Who makes your choices? Your boss? Your spouse? Your stomach?

If you finish a meal and say to yourself, "I can't believe I ate so much. I didn't intend to," it's your stomach making your choices.

If you purchase something you really didn't want because it looked appealing in the advertisement, the advertisers are making your choices.

The way to make your own choices is to define your life by principles and stick to them consistently until you have formed a habit.

Start today.

Write down one new habit you want to form within yourself.

Phrase it as a life principle.

Memorize it and repeat it to yourself often throughout the day.

Practice it consistently for 30 days.

Then look back and take stock of your life.

You will be amazed how your life can improve when you make your own choices.

Plan Your Work and Work Your Plan

An ancient Chinese proverb says, "The longest journey begins with one step." That's not entirely true. A successful journey begins with some planning and a map that tells you how to reach your destination. Then, you take your first step.

Norman Vincent Peale, author of *The Power of Positive Thinking* was fond of saying, "Plan your work for today and every day, then work your plan." [24]

Always begin your day with a plan. Developing your plan after you've started is too late. You will spend your first hour flailing around and then spend the rest of the day trying to formulate a plan as interruptions and distractions continually draw you away. Sure, even with a plan, you will be challenged by interruptions, distractions, emergencies, or the boss's immediate requests.

Your plan gives you something to go back to. It quickly gets you back on track after you have "put the fire out."

Take the last 10 minutes of your workday to plan the next day.

Having a carefully developed plan applies to everyone. As a writer and consultant, my work is a little different. I spend about an hour each day in prayer and meditation. At the close of that meditation time, I jot down ideas and plans of what I want to accomplish each day. A musician should approach every practice session with a plan. Ideally, every practice should include technical work such as scales or vocalises, sight-reading, improvisation, and rehearsal of specific pieces for performance. Parents certainly need a plan for dealing with children and their activities.

Work out your own planning schedule, but make it a priority. Do it every day.

Not all the planning and preparation in the world will get you to your destination unless you move and do something. If you focus too much on long-range goals that seem insurmountable, you may feel overwhelmed. Use long-range goals as a vision to inspire you to keep moving. Be mindful of upcoming activities so you can plan and prepare for them. But focus on the task at hand. Every objective is accomplished one step at a time.

We will discuss developing an action plan in Chapter 7.

Which Comes First: Immediate or Important?

Many people live in (and many companies operate in) "crisis mode." They become so distracted by the tyranny of the immediate, that they completely lose sight of the important. If they continue in that mode long enough their days will soon be dictated by the urgent. In other words, they exist in "crisis mode."

Golda Meir was prime minister of Israel during the Yom Kippur War and the Munich Olympic team attack. She was no stranger to crisis. She put it this way, "I must govern the clock, not be governed by it."

A Health Example

When Hippocrates was defining the medical profession in the fifth century BC, he insisted that maintaining health was more important than repairing injury or disease.[25] Ask people today what doctors are for and many will tell you that doctors fix sick people. Few think of physicians as health guides. With that thinking, we tend to ignore what is important until it becomes an immediate crisis.

Some issues are both immediate and important, such as a serious illness. These tend to get the most attention. Others are immediate but not so important, such as, "I'm hungry now." Still others are important, but not immediate: "I want to eat healthy meals and exercise daily."

Doctors estimate that 80% of all disease-related deaths could have been prevented if proper nutrition and exercise regimens had been followed for ten years preceding the onset of the disease. That should encourage all of us to wake up and avoid the crisis.

Do you prioritize your life and time like this?

Priority 1: Immediate and Important

"I think I'm having a heart attack."

Priority 2: Immediate but not Important

"It's lunchtime. I'm hungry. I'll just go buy get some fast food."

Priority 3: Important but not Immediate

"I should get up earlier so I can exercise and fix a healthy meal to take for lunch."

Obviously, immediate and important issues must be taken care of first. However, placing more emphasis on issues that are important but not yet immediate will help prevent us from being driven by crisis.

Some Business Examples

- If an account executive doesn't take time to do proper follow up with a client, he will soon be in

140

"crisis mode," trying to save the account or replace a lost client.

- If a manager doesn't take time to notice and reward good performance, he will soon be in "crisis mode," having to hire and train new employees.
- If a technician doesn't take time to study and stay current with the newest technologies, he will soon be in "crisis mode," looking for a new job.

Don't just be efficient with your time; be effective with your time.

Priorities are as Simple as A-B-C

Before each day begins, make a list of everything you want to achieve. It's a simple "To Do" list. Prioritize as A, B or C.

A= Very important and immediate.
B = Very important but not immediate.
C = Important long-term goal.

Check off items as you accomplish them. Add new items as you think of them during the day. Review your list at the close of each day.

Focus on your B goals. Allocate sacred devoted time to your C goals. Your A goals will be so demanding that you won't be able to forget about them. Don't worry; you will get your A's done. But, if you focus on your A's, your B's will be left undone until they become A's and your C's will never be considered.

It's your B's that make your life easier and more peaceful. By focusing on your B's, you will prevent them from becoming A's. Your tasks will be done before they become critical. It's like preventative medicine. But it's your C's that will get you to your long-term goals. Allocate dedicated time to their accomplishment and smile at the end of each day, knowing you are moving forward toward the fulfillment of your life vision.

Risk - Issue - Opportunity Management

Be a yardstick of quality. Some people aren't used to an environment where excellence is expected.
- Steve Jobs

Shaklee Corporation is a leading producer of natural nutritional supplementation products. They maintain their leadership by having the strictest quality control standards of anyone in the industry. Shaklee conducts over 100,000 quality control tests annually on raw materials for product consistency and effectiveness. They have conducted over 100 clinical studies, the majority of which have been published in peer-reviewed journals. They test all natural raw materials used for 350 contaminants including pesticides, herbicides, heavy metals, and solvent residues.[26] As a result, Shaklee has never been successfully sued for quality issues with their products. Other similar companies have paid out millions of dollars for serious side effects and even wrongful death. Shaklee's policy of getting it right before the product reaches the consumer may cost in the short term, but pays huge dividends in the long term. That's why Shaklee's products were chosen for both the Biosphere and NASA's Space Shuttle program.

Typical business consultants approach risk management with a variety of insurance options. The forward thinking businessperson covers potentially fatal business issues with proper insurance coverage. Businesses are insured against personal injury liability, fire, theft, errors and omissions, disability or death of principals, and a host of other events that could potentially drive a small business concern out of business.

A growing number of business consultants are looking at risk management as extending beyond insurance to a business culture that anticipates and avoids risk. It 's called "Risk - Issue - Opportunity Management" and has four keystones:

1. Identify the risks inherent with your business or location.
2. Focus on the root cause of the risk rather than its symptoms or consequences.
3. Develop a risk-reduction plan, with concrete and scheduled action steps to reduce risk.
4. Include funding of risk avoidance instead of just planning to pay for things when they go wrong.

Resources Within You

To the mind that is still, the whole universe surrenders.
- Lao Tzu

Earlier we discussed two key resources of time and money. But, you may tell me, "I am a single parent, working two jobs to keep a roof over my head and food on the table. I don't have any time or money to make something better in my life. I am in survival mode."

Nelson failed his senior year in college, was branded a communist, and sentenced to hard labor for life in prison. His eyesight was permanently damaged by long days working in the bright sunlight. Yet, he maintained hope and developed what resources were available to him. He memorized poetry. He fostered friendships with the guards. He wrote an autobiography, which he smuggled out of the prison. While maintaining his personal identity as a Christian, he studied the religions of other prisoners so he could relate to them better. Still, his 70th birthday found him suffering from tuberculosis in solitary confinement. As his internment finally eased, Nelson finished his degree via correspondence. Following intense international pressure, he was released from prison. Many might slip quietly into retirement at the age of 71 after over 27 years of imprisonment, but Nelson Mandela continued to use what he learned of universal resources to be elected President of South Africa, end the nation's racial apartheid policy, and win the Nobel Peace Prize.

Your success and fulfillment in life is not limited by how much money is in your bank account or how many exotic vacations you're able to take. Even if you have no readily accessible time or money, you can still move toward the fulfillment of your life vision by learning to tap into universal resources available within you. These are resources that belong to everyone and that link everyone together. They are, in the end, more powerful than time or money.

Even if you have neither time nor money, you can still enjoy success in your life. Remember our definition of success in the first chapter? *Success is receiving satisfaction and fulfillment from an endeavor you are truly passionate about.* Receiving financial compensation for that endeavor is a necessity for most of us. The good news is that financial reward is a byproduct of being truly successful. There are several universal resources available to you regardless of your current situation that can help move you toward your life vision. Develop these resources and your life will grow steadily, even if slowly at times, toward a more fulfilling and rewarding future.

When you have absolutely nothing except the universal resources that lie deep inside your soul, you can still accomplish great things if you focus on what you have instead of what you don't have.

Happiness

Sow the seeds of happiness in others, and you will reap a joyful harvest.
- Dr. Forrest C. Shaklee, Sr.

It's a little-known fact that happy people are more successful at what they do and even make more money. We tend to think we want to be successful so we can be happy. But the reality is the other way around. If we are happy, we will attract more success. Researchers at the University of California, Riverside reviewed 225 subject articles in a variety of psychology journals and became convinced that happiness brings success, not vice versa.[27]

Do you prefer to be around happy people or gloomy people?

Do you prefer to go shopping at a store where the owner and sales people remember your name and are glad to see you? Or do you prefer to go to stores where the employees are unhappy or even angry?

Suppose you were interviewing two people for a position in your company. The first had a positive outlook and impressed you as a fun person to be around. The second was sullen and made you feel uncomfortable. Whom would you hire?

Happiness begins inside, and then works its way outside. Events in life do not make us happy or unhappy. It's how we react to those events that determines our disposition. American commentator Andy Rooney put it this way, "Happiness depends more on how life strikes you than on what happens."

When life throws you a curve ball, knock it out of the park.

Happiness attracts success. It helps you have a positive attitude and makes you more enjoyable to be around.

Smile

Psychologist Robert Zajonc published a fascinating study on the power of smiling. He didn't tell the research subjects that the research was about smiling. Instead, he had them repeat vowel sounds and note their emotional state before and after uttering the vowel. What he discovered was that repeating "ee" made people happy and repeating "oo" made people sad. The reason is that "ee" creates a smile, and "oo" creates a pout.[28]

Psychologists Hertenstein, Hansel, Butts, and Hile reviewed hundreds of photos from university yearbooks. In some, individuals smiled broadly and freely. Others barely smiled or presented fake smiles. Still others looked very unhappy to be having their picture taken. The team of psychologists evaluated the smiles in the photos and rated them in degrees of smile. They then followed up on the individuals and discovered that those with frowns or fake smiles were significantly more likely to get divorced.[29] Smiling is not the key to a happy marriage, but it is indicative of emotional balance and contentment necessary for positive interpersonal relationships.

Other research has indicated that people who routinely share a genuine smile are likely to live longer and survive better in crisis.

Are you smiling today?

Self-Confidence

A story is told of a businessman who never seemed to be able to get ahead. Sales were lackluster. His deals kept falling through. He was badly in debt. As he was taking a walk in Central Park, all he could think about was impending bankruptcy. He sat on a bench with his head in his hands, feeling like it was the end of the world. An old man sat beside him and struck up a conversation.

"You seem to be troubled."

"I just can't do anything right. My business is failing. I'm about to declare bankruptcy. I guess I'm just not cut out for business."

"Let me see if I can help," the old man mused. He reached into his pocket, drew out his checkbook, and wrote a check. "Here, see if this helps. All I ask is that you meet me here on this bench exactly one year from today and pay me back."

As the old man walked away, the businessman looked down at the check. It was for one million dollars and signed by John D. Rockefeller.

The businessman was elated as he walked straight to his bank. However, he thought better of the idea and decided to put the check in his safe. "I'll know it's there if I really need it."

Amazingly, things turned around for the businessman. He approached new deals with confidence, knowing he had a million dollars in his safe if he needed it. Sales continued to climb as the businessman stopped appearing desperate, but approached customers with confidence.

When the year was up, the businessman was now successful and on top of the world. He proudly went to the park bench to return the check and explain how it had given him the confidence to build a successful business. When he reached the bench, there was the same old man, only this time there was a nurse sitting next to him.

"Mr. Rockefeller...," the businessman began. But the nurse interrupted him. "Oh, he's not John Rockefeller. He keeps wandering away from the nursing home telling people that. I hope he hasn't been bothering you."

The moral is simple. Confidence in yourself and your business is your greatest asset - and may be the only asset you need.

If you believe in yourself, you will attract more success. Who wants to promote a worker who doesn't believe in himself? Who wants to buy a product from a sales person who lacks confidence in his own product? Who wants to marry a person who doesn't think he or she is capable of being a great spouse? You will never be successful unless others believe in you. If you want others to believe in you, you must first believe in yourself.

Compelling Vision

If your actions inspire others to dream more, learn more,
do more, and become more, you are a leader.
- John Quincy Adams

Mother Theresa had a vision to help the poorest of the poor.
She took a vow of poverty and lived among the poor of
Calcutta, India. She devoted her life to the sick, the
penniless, and the dying. Her vision was so compelling that
thousands lined up to help fulfill her vision. At the time of
her death, over 4,000 Missionaries of Charity were devoted
to fulfilling her vision, and her order controlled over
$40,000,000, mostly in real estate owned in 133 countries,
for the purpose of caring for the poorest of the poor. Not
bad for someone who personally never owned more than
two saris and a bucket to wash them in. Her compelling
vision served as her mustard seed.

Do you know where you want to go in life? Is it real? Is it
compelling?

Consider the 2008 presidential election. Who offered the
more compelling vision? Both candidates ran on a platform
of "Change." But Obama created a public perception of
change and actually imparted a compelling vision. For all
McCain's talk about change, he was perceived as more of
the same.

I would even propose that corporate marketing, at its best,
is all about imparting a compelling vision. I remember
McDonald's ad campaign during the family friendly 80's,
which showed the clown inspiring father and son, mother
and daughter, complete with musical score that could only
be described as inspirational. Suddenly, parents had to take
their children to McDonald's in order to be perceived as

good parents. Millions stood in line to propel McDonald's Corporation to their vision of being number one in the fast food industry. Forget the fat, sugar, and sodium.

What makes your vision compelling to others?

First, state your vision clearly if you want to compel others to join your cause. People will not follow a vague proposition. They need to understand where your vision is leading and how it will benefit them.

Second, for your vision to compel others it must be identifiable. People need to identify with your vision. They will follow a vision that they feel is theirs as well as yours.

Third, your vision must offer hope. Hope is your greatest gift. Stir hope in the hearts of those who would follow your vision, and you will not lack for support in fulfilling your goals.

A compelling vision will attract people and resources to help you get there. The more vivid and compelling your vision, the more people and resources will line up to propel you to your goal.

Expand Your Resources

Trust yourself. Create the kind of self that you will be happy to live with all your life. Make the most of yourself by fanning the tiny, inner sparks of possibility into flames of achievement.
- Golda Meir

What do you need to help you achieve your goal? Is it a higher degree? Experience? A coach or mentor? Is it an essential stepping-stone, or are you just lacking self-confidence?

Make a mental map of how you're going to reach your destination. What will you need for your journey? What will you need when you get there? Think it through. What is the first step? The next step? Chart it out. Put it on paper. See your map. Read it aloud. You will notice different things that need adjustment when you read it aloud. You may think of some steps you missed. You may rearrange certain steps.

Collect the resources you need. Sometimes the resources are sub-goals you must achieve before you can act on your larger goal.

- Get the degree you need.
- Create your network of friends and supporters.
- Gain experience in your chosen field.
- Ally yourself to a mentor who will train and equip you.

Be careful not to allow the lack of a resource to be an excuse to give up on your dream. Having an MBA can be a great asset if you're pursuing success in business. But there are thousands of successful business people who do not have MBAs. Bill Gates didn't even have his college degree when he started Microsoft, and he went on to become the richest man in the world.

Guided Meditation: Looking Back

A CD of this meditation is available from Amazon.com and other retail outlets.

Find a place where you will not be observed or disturbed.

Sit up straight in a comfortable position.

Close your eyes.

Allow yourself to breathe naturally. Take breath in. Let breath out.

Now take a deep cleansing breath in through your nose, if possible. Notice the rise and fall of your chest and abdomen. Notice the sense of chill as cool air passes through your nostrils. Blow it all out, pushing up with your diaphragm to empty your lungs completely. Take a second cleansing breath to rejuvenate your lungs with fresh air.

Take a few upper breaths, focusing on pushing the air into the chest portion of your lungs. Take your fingertips and touch your heart. Feel your chest move up and down as you take each breath. Breathe in, through your nose if possible, and out through your mouth. If you can't breathe that way, don't worry. That technique is just a way to help take your mind off other things and concentrate on your breath.

Now take a few lower breaths, focusing on pushing air as deeply into your abdomen as possible. Again, breathe in, through your nose if possible, and out through your mouth. As you inhale, imagine yourself breathing in positive energy. As you exhale, imagine yourself breathing out negative energy. Say to yourself:

Breathe in peace; breathe out anxiety.
Breathe in faith; breathe out doubt.
Breathe in love; breathe out indifference.
Breathe in hope; breathe out despair.
Breathe in confidence; breathe out timidity.

Empty your mind of feelings of stress or anxiety. Thoughts about problems at work or home may rush in at this point. That's normal. Don't fight the thoughts. Just acknowledge them and let them slip away.

Relax your body. Focus on your head. Recognize any tension in your scalp, face, or jaw. Will each area to relax. Let your jaw slip down slightly into a relaxed position. Now focus on your neck and shoulders. Again, recognize any tension and will each area to relax. Repeat this relaxation technique for your arms and chest. As you focus on your diaphragm, your breathing may alter a bit. You may begin to breathe a little more deeply and regularly as if asleep. Continue the technique, moving down your body until you reach your toes. Take a moment to realize that you are fully relaxed.

See yourself at least ten years older than you are now. You're seated in a comfortable chair behind the oversized desk in your study, or perhaps the kitchen table of your dream home. All around you is tidy with your favorite photos adorning the walls. Opposite you sits a journalist who is writing your life's story. She asks you what you consider to be your top three greatest accomplishments. These are the top three things you have accomplished between today and this imaginary event, which takes place at least 10 years in the future. You mull it over in your mind for a minute, and then list your top accomplishments.

Write them down.

_____

_____

_____

Now the journalist asks you how you achieved the first of your top three accomplishments. Again, you mull that over for a moment and then briefly outline how you managed that feat.

Write down the basic steps you took to achieve your top accomplishment.

_____

_____

_____

Now the journalist asks you how you fulfilled the second of your most important accomplishments. Again, you mull that over for a moment and then briefly outline how you performed that feat.

Write down the basic steps you took to achieve your second most important accomplishment.

_____

_____

_____

Now the journalist asks you how you achieved your third most important accomplishment. Again, you mull that over for a moment and then briefly outline how you accomplished that feat.

Write down the basic steps you took to achieve your third most important accomplishment.

_____

_____

_____

Take a moment to consider all you have accomplished in the last 10 or more years. Focus on your sense of pride and accomplishment. You're not only proud of what you have done, you're proud of yourself.

While focusing on that sense of self-love and pride, take a few deep breaths.

Open your eyes and return to the present, fully aware and confident of what your future holds.

Notes from Your Guided Meditation

_____

_____

_____

_____

_____

_____

_____

_____

_____

_____

_____

_____

_____

CHAPTER 7

Action Steps Take You to Your Goals

Do you want to know who you are? Don't ask. Act! Action will delineate and define you.
- Thomas Jefferson

Now we get to where the rubber meets the road: Formulate a plan of action steps that will get you where you want to be.

If you're a student, what degree would best move you forward in your chosen career? What summer jobs or internships would look best on your resume? Can you foster relationships or begin correspondence with individuals who might help you get started?

If you're in sales, how are you going to gather your prospects? What are you going to say? What will your contact media be? When was the last time you updated your presentation? How do you plan to close? What about follow up? It all needs to be in your plan.

Perhaps you're a business owner ready to take your company or product to the next level of renown and profits. How are you going to make that happen? Does your business plan specifically cover growth like this? How can you expand your client-base?

If you're a parent whose last child recently left the nest, is now the time to launch the nonprofit organization you've dreamed of for decades? Do you know how to start a nonprofit? Do you have influential supporters lined up? How do you intend to get the message out to the masses?

Walk It Backwards

Once you know your life vision and have identified the ultimate goals that will enable your life vision, break it down - backwards. It's a great way to outline the steps you need to take to accomplish your ultimate goals that fulfill your life vision. You can also use this exercise for shorter-term goals that lead to your ultimate goals.

It's best to begin with a five-year plan. Some simple endeavors can use a three-year plan. Long-term goals that are more complex may require a ten-year plan. But you should be able to accomplish just about anything in 10 years. Remember, we got a man on the moon within 10 years of President Kennedy declaring the race to space.

First, create a mental image of you having accomplished an ultimate goal. Write it down. This picture should be a part of the life vision you created in Chapter 3.

Now, imagining that you are in the future, think of what you did just before accomplishing that ultimate goal. What did you do before that? Keep listing the steps backwards until you get to where you are today.

So, what is the first step to take now? It's the last step you listed working backwards from the future to the present. It is the beginning of your plan. Look over my example that follows. Then, write your own process backwards.

Example: My Ultimate Goal
Write a book to help people find their way through the transitions of life.

Vision: I am enjoying the success of my new book "*Where Do I Go from Here?*" I have a never-ending stream of requests for speaking engagements. I am having a blast at book signings around the country. I am able to combine speaking engagements, book signings, and a little vacation in each trip. All this is fun, but the most rewarding part of the experience is the feedback I receive from thousands of readers who have truly been helped by my book. They are the true purpose of my writing.

Steps to reach the goal in reverse order. Each step cannot be reached until the preceding step is complete. (Notice they are written as affirmations in the present tense.)

16. I am drawing on a well-established network of friends and acquaintances to secure frequent speaking engagements and book signings. Sales continue to grow exponentially as more and more people are helped by the principles and meditations in the book.
15. I am placing my first order for 1,000 print copies of my book.
14. I am performing the final edit of my book and adding endorsements from my pre-publication edition.
13. I am sending pre-publication editions of my book to selected readers for endorsements.
12. I am selecting a book publisher and arranging for a small printing for pre-publication.
11. I am performing multiple rewrites of my book. This step gets boring, but I remember Mohamed Ali's words, "I hated every minute of training. But I kept telling myself, 'Work hard now, and live the rest of your life as a champion.'"

---

10. I am putting the final changes on my expanded book. Now, the rewrites begin.

9. I am writing consistently, putting at least one hour a day into an expanded version of my book.

8. I am reviewing the testimonials I have received from those who have used my book, refining my principles and processes for the expanded print edition.

7. I am doing three to four webinars a week marketing my new book. Sales are doing well.

6. I am publishing my initial public version as an eBook.

5. I am reworking the book based on comments and feedback from friends and colleagues who read the pre-published version.

4. I am giving pre-published copies of my book to friends and colleagues for comment and feedback.

3. I am writing consistently, putting at least an hour a day into my success workbook.

2. I am developing and practicing the *Stillness* techniques that are the unique feature of my book.

1. I am researching the many gurus of success. What do they have in common? What is just pie in the sky, and what is truly practical? What has worked for me? What is working for me now? Do these principles produce consistent results?

The next worksheet will help you chart a plan to reach *your* goal.

160

Walking It Backwards

My Ultimate Goal:

_____

The Last Step:

_____

Before that:

10. _____

9. _____

8. _____

7. _____

6. _____

5. _____

4. _____

3. _____

2. _____

1. _____

Create a Realistic and Flexible Timeline

Learn from the past, set vivid, detailed goals for the future, and live in the only moment of time over which you have any control: now.
- Denis Waitley

As you outline the steps, it is natural to begin creating a timeline in your head for when these steps can be accomplished. One common mistake is to attach unrealistic timeframes to lofty goals. We live in a world of fast food, microwaves, high-speed transport, and 90-second sound bites. We have come to expect everything instantly. It seems reasonable that we should be promoted to vice-president in two years, start our own company in five years, and retire a millionaire in 10 years. It has happened before. It will happen again. But are you in a position to pursue that path?

Often what is possible is only realistic if achieving your goal is the only thing you have to do in life. The complexities of life must be taken into account. Do you have a spouse? Children? Friends? Involvements in church or civic organizations? Most people are busy before they launch into the new endeavor that will propel them to actualize their life vision.

Break your goals down into simple, realistic, achievable, and measureable steps. Create a realistic timeline projecting when those steps can be accomplished. Be flexible with your plan. Steps will change as you move along your path. Interruptions will happen. They can slow you down, but don't let them stop you.

As I mentioned before, keep your ultimate vision in your mind's eye to inspire you to stay on track. Focus on accomplishing short-term goals that move you forward in the right direction. For instance, where do you want to be in 90 days that will move you toward your ultimate objective? How will you get there? Focus on what you will do today to move you closer to the fulfillment of your life vision.

Regardless of how near or distant your destination is, your journey will be taken one step at a time.

Recapping Key Concepts

Here are the four key concepts we have discussed so far. Use these to develop your plan for ultimate success.

1.   Vision
2.   Goals
3.   Action Steps
4.   Timeline

Let's do a quick recap here.

Your vision is *your* mental image of success - where you want to be at the end of this journey. It is sometimes referred to as your life vision. Where you want to live. What lifestyle you want to enjoy. What people you want to be with. What income you want to have. And any other success measurement you ultimately want to achieve. Your vision is very long term and can adjust over time as your life and interests change.

Your goals are realistic, achievable results. They can be components of your ultimate vision or steps along the way. Your ultimate goal is that aspect of your life vision that you are directly working to achieve. It makes other aspects of your life vision possible. For example, your life vision may include living on a horse farm or having freedom for leisure travel. Your ultimate goal might be owning a thriving business, becoming a bestselling author, achieving the top sales rank in your company, or rising to the position of CEO of a nationally known corporation. The income generated from achieving your ultimate goal makes your life vision possible. Sub-goals or milestone goals are measureable accomplishments along the way that keep you on track as you work to fulfill your ultimate goal and life vision.

Your action steps are the activities you do to keep you moving forward on the journey. If you're in sales, an action step would be the number of phone calls you need to make to get the appointments you need to reach your sales goal. A sale is not an action step, since a sale is not under your control. Number of sales per month is a goal. Number of phone calls per day is an action step.

The timeframe is a realistic estimate of when your ultimate goal and/or sub-goals will be accomplished. In other words, how long will it realistically take to achieve your goals? Your timeline is an estimated schedule for the completion of the action steps that will lead you to the accomplishment of your goals. Like any schedule, your timeline may change, as circumstances require.

Your Action Steps Must be Under Your Control

If you are unemployed, finding a job may be a goal, but it cannot be an action step because you cannot hire yourself. Sending resumes, making follow up phone calls, contacting recruiters, attending networking events, and getting up-to-date certifications are all action steps to move you closer to your goal of getting a job.

The action steps are under your control, so there is no excuse for not accomplishing them. You will have the opportunity to develop your own action plan in Chapter 8.

A Home-Based Business Example

My wife has a successful network marketing business. I have been privileged to watch her vision become more of a reality every year because she understands the concept of vision/goals/action steps. Without using her specific goals, let's just look at one way she has moved forward in her business.

For our example, we'll pretend you are in business with her.

Define your Ultimate Goal

Say you want to earn $200,000 a year in your business, live in your dream home, and drive your dream car. That's your vision.

Break it Down

When broken down, and based on realistic expectations of your company's sales plan, you should be earning $1,000 a month by the end of your first year. For that to happen, what do your product sales need to be? How many organizational leaders do you need to develop? Your answers here are your goals. And remember, every goal needs to be SMART (**S**pecific, **M**otivating, **A**ccountable, **R**ealistic, and **T**ough). How are you going to reach your goals? Will you make a list of your friends and family and talk to them about your new business? Purchase leads? Meet with strangers you've connected with through local or online networking groups? Will you publish a monthly newsletter to inform and generate interest? Hold in-home parties or rent space at local events? Do product demonstrations? Looking at these types of questions, you can see a plan coming together, right? The answers to these questions are your action steps.

As you develop your plan, you will see some overlap between goals and action steps. This is particularly true of short-term goals. A goal of talking to 10 people about your product each day may also be an action step. A longer-term goal, such as earning a company paid trip, is clearly the culmination of many action steps along the way.

Next, ask yourself if you are willing and able to do what it takes to follow the plan? That's your commitment level. If you answer in the negative, adjust your goal or your timeframe.

Many people have a full time job and embark on a business like this to earn some extra income. It's easy to be swept away by the promises of six-figure incomes and fancy trips, but then get discouraged when you can't put the time into your new business to make those things happen as quickly as you want.

Whether you're starting a business from home or building the next Fortune 500 Empire, realistically assess your time and investment potential. Develop powerful action steps that will move you toward your goals. If you can only commit three hours a week to a home-based business, you can still succeed. The trick is to remain consistent with your time investment commitment as well as keeping faithful to your plan.

Develop and Define Monthly, Weekly, and Daily Goals

Discipline is the bridge between goals and accomplishment.
- Jim Rohn

Monthly
- The average product user buys $100 of product each month, so I need to add 10 product users each month.
- One out of every three product demonstrations results in a new product user, so I need to do product demonstrations to 30 people a month.
- Using the party method, I am in front of an average of five people per party, so I need to do six parties a month.

Weekly
- I will schedule two parties a week because some will cancel.
- As potential future sales leaders become apparent, I will provide weekly training and coaching to those in my down-line who decide to build their own businesses.

Daily
- I will talk to 200 people to find one who will persevere to become a sales leader. I can easily do that contacting 10 people per day, either in person or on the phone.

Define the Action Steps You Will Take to Realize Your Vision

Now that you have determined where you want to go, list the steps it will take you to get there. Continuing with the network-marketing example, a checklist might look something like this:

- Make a list of my friends, relatives, and acquaintances.
- Contact each person on my list to let him or her know what I am doing. Personally contact 10 people each day. No secrets or ulterior motives. Just let them know what I am becoming involved with and ask them if they would like to host a party.
- Schedule two parties a week.
- At each party, offer incentives for attendees to schedule two additional parties.
- Set up a tickler system to contact each customer monthly and ask for repeat business.
- Begin a blog to discuss my industry. Write weekly. Become known as an expert in my field.
- Create social media accounts to enlarge my sphere of influence.
- Call each person who has ordered more than once and offer to visit one on one to go over distributorship program.
- Develop organizational leaders through weekly training meetings for new distributors.
- Achieve the next rank in my parent company.

Check Your Time

Does you plan fit in the amount of time you have to give it? Be sure to allow time for family, friends, and recreation. Otherwise, pursuit of your goal can become a burden you resent, not a joyful experience that empowers you.

Since most people get involved in a home-based business part time, the plan outlined previously fits into a 20 hour per week timeframe. Some people may have only 5-10 hours a week for this endeavor, so they will need to adjust their plan.

If the plan doesn't support the goal, you may need to adjust the goal. OR, just learn to work smarter. Use of advertising or the Internet can leverage your time. But the key here is make sure you have the time to devote to your plan. If not, make some adjustments or you will just become frustrated.

Adjust as You Move Along

Re-evaluate your plan every 30 to 90 days. You may need to change your approach, your technique, or your tools. Periodically you will want to revisit your long-term goal. Is that still your goal? Have changes in life caused you to reconsider? That's okay. These are your goals. You can make them whatever you please.

Always test and refine your process. But watch out for the trap of trying to find the perfect process. It doesn't exist. Some things just don't work and need to be dropped. Most things work if you do them well enough and often enough. But few things work as well as we wish they did. I will talk more about score keeping in chapter 10. For now, just be aware that all you need is a percentage of success for each activity. Whatever the percentage is, you can use it to formulate your plan.

Focus on the Principle

Remember, this is not a book about network marketing or any other home-based business, but about principles that will help you succeed regardless of your endeavor. Many people are getting involved in network marketing, even Donald Trump, Warren Buffet, and Roger Barnett. Because of my wife's experience and success in network marketing,

I chose examples from her work to illustrate how to develop a plan.

You can apply these principles no matter your goal—be it building a profitable car wash or becoming the next great chess master.

- Decide where you want to go.
- Break it down into measurable accomplishments along the way.
- Plan simple action steps you can begin tomorrow that will get you there.

Keep these principles in mind and have a good journey.

Goal Worksheet

Today's Date: _____

5 Year Goal

_____

1 Year Goal

_____

3 Month Goal

_____

1 Month Goal

_____

This Week's Goal

_____

Three Things I Choose to do Today to Move Me Closer to My Goal

1. _____

2. _____

3. _____

Guided Meditation:
You Have Arrived

A CD of this meditation is available from Amazon.com and other retail outlets.

Find a place where you will not be observed or disturbed.

Sit up straight in a comfortable position.

Close your eyes.

Allow yourself to breathe naturally. Take breath in. Let breath out.

Now take a deep cleansing breath in through your nose, if possible. Notice the rise and fall of your chest and abdomen. Notice the sense of chill as the cool air passes through your nostrils. Blow it all out, pushing up with your diaphragm to empty your lungs completely. Take a second cleansing breath to rejuvenate your lungs with fresh air.

Take a few upper breaths, focusing on pushing the air into the chest portion of your lungs. Take your fingertips and touch your heart. Feel your chest move up and down as you take each breath. Breathe in, through your nose if possible, and out through your mouth. If you can't breathe that way, don't worry. That technique is just a way to help take your mind off other things and concentrate on your breath.

Now take a few lower breaths, focusing on pushing air as deeply into your abdomen as possible. Again, breathe in, through your nose if possible, and out through your mouth. As you inhale, imagine yourself breathing in positive

energy. As you exhale, imagine yourself breathing out negative energy. Say to yourself:

> *Breathe in peace; breathe out anxiety.*
> *Breathe in faith; breathe out doubt.*
> *Breathe in love; breathe out indifference.*
> *Breathe in hope; breathe out despair.*
> *Breathe in confidence; breathe out timidity.*

Empty your mind of feelings of stress or anxiety. Thoughts about problems at work or home may rush in at this point. That's normal. Don't fight the thoughts. Just acknowledge them and let them slip away.

Relax your body. Focus on your head. Recognize any tension in your scalp, face, or jaw. Will each area to relax. Let your jaw slip down slightly into a relaxed position. Now focus on your neck and shoulders. Again, recognize any tension and will each area to relax. Repeat this relaxation technique for your arms and chest. As you focus on your diaphragm, your breathing may alter a bit. You may begin to breathe a little more deeply and regularly as if asleep. Continue the technique, moving down your body until you reach your toes. Take a moment to realize that you are fully relaxed.

You have arrived. You have set your goals. You have determined your plan. You have worked your plan. There have been setbacks, but you overcame them all. You are now living the life of your dreams.

Picture in your mind the house you live in. What does it look like? Where is it located? Imagine walking into your entranceway. Take in the sights, smells, and feel of your dream home.

Imagine your daily activities. What are you doing each day? How does it all make you feel?

Now ask yourself, "How did I get here? What opportunities did I seek? What decisions led me to this moment? What obstacles did I overcome? How did I overcome them? What did I give up to get here? Was it worth it?"

Take a moment to focus on the sense of pride and accomplishment of having achieved what you set out to do. You're in the top 1% of the population. You have a right to be proud.

Take a deep breath. Let it all out. Open your eyes and remember that sense of pride and accomplishment you just felt.

Take a moment to jot down some notes of what you discovered about your journey.

Notes from Your Guided Meditation

_____

_____

_____

_____

_____

_____

_____

_____

_____

_____

_____

_____

_____

CHAPTER 8

Realistic Milestones Keep You on Track

If you want to make your dreams come true, the first thing you have to do is wake up.
-J.M. Power

A project manager looks at the big picture and compartmentalizes it into small manageable functions. For example, if the project is to build a house, the project manager names the functions that would include:

1. Select house plan
2. Collect bids
3. Grade the lot
4. Pour the foundation
5. Frame out the house
6. Rough in plumbing and electrical
7. Finish exterior work
8. Paint
9. Install flooring
10. Install cabinetry and complete finish carpentry

The project manager then puts every function on a Gantt chart, which is a specialized type of timeline that ensures everything is done in order and as efficiently as possible. Some steps may overlap. Others must be completed before the next step can begin. You wouldn't want to lay the carpet before you finished the roof, or do the finish carpentry before you paint. As each function is finished, milestones are met, and the next function begins.

Be Your Own Project Manager

Your journey to your goal requires some project management. Whatever your goal is, it will probably take some time and effort to accomplish. Plan your journey step by step. If your goal is to own a chain of restaurants, you might begin by managing a restaurant for someone else to learn the trade. You then develop a business plan, find a location, procure financing, commence construction, hire a staff, order inventory, launch your marketing program, open your doors, and develop operational systems so the restaurant runs smoothly without your constant involvement. You will likely make many adjustments during the first couple of years. You might adjust your menu, décor, and food preparation systems. After two years of profitability, it will be time to search for a second location.

Each step is a milestone that should be measurable, verifiable, and celebrated. Then begin working toward the next milestone.

Know Your Objectives

The battlefield commander is constantly moving toward objectives. Take the hill. Secure the bridge. Garrison the town. He must be very clear on what he must accomplish because lives are at stake.

There are many objectives on the path to your goal. Know what they are. Your life vision is at stake.

Every profession has its own steps, like rungs on a ladder. An attorney starts out as a junior associate, then associate, junior partner, and finally full partner.

What are the steps to the top of your profession? Make the
list and create a realistic timeline for the accomplishment
each step.

What will it take to reach each step?

How long will it take to reach them?

If you want to be at the top in five years, what level do you
want to reach in one year?

What do you need to accomplish in the next six months to
be halfway to that objective?

What will you accomplish in the next month to ensure you
are well on your way?

What can you do this week to get you started?

If you need to, go back and review the Walking It
Backwards exercise in Chapter 7.

***You should know your objectives for one year from now,
six months from now and one month from now. Plus, you
should know what you're going to do this week to keep
you moving in the right direction.***

Track Your Goals

There are no shortcuts to any place worth going.
- Beverly Sills

You wrote down your ultimate goals in Chapter 2. You
determined the steps you needed to accomplish to reach
your goals in Chapter 7. In this chapter, you will create a
way to monitor your progress.

Now you want to develop a clear Plan of Action. Use it to plan your path to your goal. Identify a milestone for each step that signifies its completion and signals the commencement of the next step. Set a projected completion date for each step.

Create a new project for this week that will keep you moving forward. Review and modify your plan weekly.

Create Incentives for Selected Milestone

Many people have a health goal to be at their ideal weight and in top condition. To accomplish big things, you must stay on track. One great way to keep you on track is to reward yourself for each milestone. It doesn't have to be expensive or fattening. Reward your hard work with an afternoon at your favorite park. Sometimes you can even get your boss to pay for your reward. I have a friend who got his boss to agree to give him $1,000 if he lost 50 pounds in six months. He lost it in four. His boss wisely reminded him that the bet was for six months so he had to keep it off for the next two months. My friend collected the money.

The path to your goal is probably hard. People without goals take all the easy, low-paying jobs. But you want to be the best. You want to be at the top of your profession. Little incentives along the way keep you moving forward.

Little incentives can pay big dividends. Be creative with yourself. Choose rewards that are meaningful to you and will inspire you to complete each step.
  - A dinner out with your spouse
  - A massage
  - A golf weekend

Rewards can grow as you approach your ultimate goal.
- A cruise with your spouse
- A family vacation
- A beach house or mountain retreat

For example, if your goal is to get an online MBA, your initial Plan of Action might look like the one below.

Action Step	Milestone	Projected Completion Date	Actual Completion Date	Reward for Completion
Review online MBA programs.	Select program.	June 6	June 4	
Make application to my chosen program.	Acceptance.	June 10	June 18	
Apply for financial aid.	Get loan.	June 30	June 28	Dinner out.

Now it is time to map out your own Plan of Action. Take the steps you outlined in Chapter 7 when you walked it backwards. Make them your action steps. For each action step, list a measurable milestone and a projected completion date. In this way you are creating the timeline we discussed in the previous chapter. Include a reward for completion where applicable. Not every action step needs a reward, but the major ones do. Rewards don't have to be expensive or fattening. A sporting event, an afternoon with your family, a fishing trip, or a spa date all make great rewards that will motivate you to keep moving forward.

My Plan of Action

Action Step	Milestone	Projected Completion Date	Actual Completion Date	Reward for Completion

Journal

In addition to a carefully laid out plan, a daily journal can be a great help to keep you on track. Your daily journal should show the short-term goal you are currently working on, individualized activities you do each day, and scheduled action steps to review in the morning. In the evening, check off action steps that were accomplished as well as list other accomplishments of the day. Don't forget to list things you are grateful for each evening to keep your attitude positive.

My Daily Journal

My action step for this week is:

_____

_____

Morning

Check List
- Practice *Stillness.*
- Read vision statement.
- Recite my affirmations.
- Review this week's action step.
- Three things I plan to accomplish today that will move me closer to my goal.

1. _____

_____

2. _____

_____

3. _____

_____

Evening

Three things I accomplished today.

1. _____

_____

2. _____

_____

3. _____

_____

Five things that I encountered or that happened today, for which I am truly grateful. (Can include accomplishments, relationships, and universal resources.)

1. _____

2. _____

3. _____

4. _____

5. _____

Guided Meditation:
Ladder of Success

A CD of this meditation is available from Amazon.com and other retail outlets.

Find a place where you will not be observed or disturbed.

Sit up straight in a comfortable position.

Close your eyes.

Allow yourself to breathe naturally. Take breath in. Let breath out.

Now take a deep cleansing breath in through your nose, if possible. Notice the rise and fall of your chest and abdomen. Notice the sense of chill as the cool air passes through your nostrils. Blow it all out, pushing up with your diaphragm to empty your lungs completely. Take a second cleansing breath to rejuvenate your lungs with fresh air.

Take a few upper breaths, focusing on pushing the air into the chest portion of your lungs. Take your fingertips and touch your heart. Feel your chest move up and down as you take each breath. Breathe in, through your nose if possible, and out through your mouth. If you can't breathe that way, don't worry. That technique is just a way to help take your mind off other things and concentrate on your breath.

Now take a few lower breaths, focusing on pushing air as deeply into your abdomen as possible. Again, breathe in, through your nose if possible, and out through your mouth. As you inhale, imagine yourself breathing in positive

energy. As you exhale, imagine yourself breathing out
negative energy. Say to yourself:

> *Breathe in peace; breathe out anxiety.*
> *Breathe in faith; breathe out doubt.*
> *Breathe in love; breathe out indifference.*
> *Breathe in hope; breathe out despair.*
> *Breathe in confidence; breathe out timidity.*

Empty your mind of feelings of stress or anxiety. Thoughts
about problems at work or home may rush in at this point.
That's normal. Don't fight the thoughts. Just acknowledge
them and let them slip away.

Relax your body. Focus on your head. Recognize any
tension in your scalp, face, or jaw. Will each area to relax.
Let your jaw slip down slightly into a relaxed position.
Now focus on your neck and shoulders. Again, recognize
any tension and will each area to relax. Repeat this
relaxation technique for your arms and chest. As you focus
on your diaphragm, you may notice your breathing change
a bit. You may begin to breathe a little more deeply and
regularly as if asleep. Continue the technique, moving
down your body until you reach your toes. Take a moment
to realize that you are fully relaxed.

As before, focus on your breath. Empty yourself of other
thoughts. Notice your sense of peace. Notice your
awareness of sounds around you. Are there other feelings
or sensations? Do you find yourself stretching or yawning?
Are there other manifestations of tension release? Whatever
your body wants to do in this state is okay. Just let yourself
relax.

Now take a deep breath and let it all out. Again.

You are standing in an open space bathed in light. In front of you is a stairway. You're not surprised to see the stairway. You were expecting it. You can look up to the top of the stairway and see your ultimate goal. Name that goal in your mind. See your goal in front of you at the top of the stairs. Your goal is real. Your goal is tangible. Your goal is achievable. Nothing can make you turn away from your goal. You are going to pursue your goal with your entire self. You're going to climb the staircase.

You take the first step. How does it feel to be that much closer to your goal? Do you know the first step to your goal? Name it to yourself now.

You take the second step. How does it feel to be that much closer to your goal? What is your second step? Name it to yourself now.

You take your third step. How does it feel to be that much closer to your goal? Do you know your third step? Name it to yourself now.

You take another step. Name it to yourself now. You have made great progress, but it has been simple because though you have always kept your eye on your ultimate goal, you only needed to focus on one step at a time.

You take another step. Name it to yourself now. How does it feel to be that much closer to your goal? Are you beginning to feel the exhilaration? Your goal is not a dream; it is a certainty.

You take another step. Name it to yourself now. How does it feel to be that much closer to your goal?

You take your final step. You have achieved your goal. How does it feel to have reached your goal? Now look down at the stairway you climbed. You never strayed. You always kept your eye on your goal.

Take a deep breath, and let it all out. Open your eyes.

Now is a good time to take some notes about the journey you have just experienced.

Notes from Your Guided Meditation

_____

_____

_____

_____

_____

_____

_____

_____

_____

_____

_____

_____

_____

CHAPTER 9

Use the Strength of Focus

When every physical and mental resource is focused, one's power to solve a problem multiplies tremendously.
- Norman Vincent Peale

Sunlight warms the Earth to an average of 57 degrees Fahrenheit. If that light is focused through a magnifying glass it can reach temperatures over 400 degrees, hot enough to light a fire. If that light is focused through a Fresnel lens, similar to those used in lighthouses, it can reach 2,000 degrees or more, hot enough to melt most metals. That's the power of focus.

Have you ever thought, "I'm smarter and more talented than that guy? How come he's making more money than me?" A common problem with very intelligent and talented people is that they have a hard time focusing. It seems that whatever they're doing is taking them away from something else they want to do or feel they should be doing. They are good at business. They are good at music. They are knowledgeable about classic movies. They like to read. They are active in three different religious and civic organizations. They are committed to their family. They are always being asked to help a friend or neighbor. And, oh yes, they have just been asked to perform in the next Community Playhouse production. They are busy and enjoy prestige and success in many areas. Why do they never reach the top in any given field? The answer is simple. They never focus.

Focus is Key to Overcoming Fear

The game has its ups and downs, but you can never lose focus of your individual goals and you can't let yourself be beat because of lack of effort.
- Michael Jordan

Have you ever watched someone that just performed an amazing act of courage be interviewed on the evening news? Perhaps they rescued a child from a burning building or dove into an icy current to pull a family from a sinking car that toppled over a bridge guardrail. The reporter usually asks, "Weren't you afraid?" And the response that usually follows is just as consistent, "I didn't have time to be afraid. I was just thinking about how much those people needed my help."

Combat veterans sometimes tremble with fear *after* the firefight is over. During the conflict, they are too busy doing their job and protecting their buddy to think about the incoming bullets.

On January 15, 2009, US Airways flight 1549 took off from New York City's La Guardia Airport headed for Charlotte, North Carolina. About two minutes after takeoff, the airliner passed through a flock of birds. In a freak occurrence, the resulting foreign object damage disabled both of the plane's engines. Captain Chesley Sullenberger, ("Sully" to his friends) immediately declared an emergency and attempted to return to La Guardia, but the aircraft was losing altitude too fast. Captain Sullenberger decided to ditch the aircraft in the Hudson River. In less than four minutes after the bird strike, he safely landed the airliner in the Hudson River. His quick action and expert piloting skills saved all on board. New York City Mayor, Michael Bloomberg awarded the entire crew the Master's Medal of the Guild of Air Pilots and Air Navigators as well as the Key to the City. Captain Sullenberger is now an inspirational and motivational speaker who travels and shares how preparation, leadership, and focus are the keys to overcoming any obstacle.[30]

That's the power of focus.

Unfinished Business Robs Your Focus

One reason so few of us achieve what we truly want is that we never direct our focus; we never concentrate our power. Most people dabble their way through life, never deciding to master anything in particular.
- Tony Robbins

Have you ever seen the sign in someone's cubicle, "A Clean Desk is a Sign of a Sick Mind?" We can all imagine what the workstation looks like. The truth is more like this: "A Clean Desk is a Sign of a Focused Mind." It is virtually impossible to focus on one project when six other unfinished projects are nagging from your peripheral vision.

In today's complex society, not many projects can be completed in only a few minutes. They may require waiting on someone else's research and input. In many organizations, even a simple memo requires several approvals before it's released. Here are a few guidelines that can help free your mind of unfinished business.

1 - Empty your inbox every day.
        If it can be done now, do it.

If it can't be done now, prioritize it, schedule it, and file it.

2 - Break large projects into small component projects that can be done at one sitting.

Hiring a new department head can take months, but the whole process can be broken down into a dozen or so bite-sized steps. Your first step might be to write a job description and email it to human resources. Put a tickler notice in your calendar to check on human resources' progress in a week, and then forget about it.

3 - Have a file for things that need to be done and review your file once a day for prioritization and scheduling. Remember to use the A-B-C method of prioritizing.

4 - Keep a file for things that require thought and consideration. Review them once a week to see if you have come up with any ideas that might move a project along.

5 - Don't belabor decisions forever. Gather the information you need, and then make the decision. You'll find the practice of *Stillness* as discussed in this book very helpful here. Clear your mind, find your peaceful place, and go with your intuition. If you are a decision maker in your company, you're there for a reason. Your intuition is really the culmination of your training and experience that resides in your subconscious. Therefore, it is free from the debilitating arguments of your rational, conscious mind. Albert Einstein was a mathematical genius, but he attributed his discovery of the theory of relativity to his intuition, not his math prowess.

6 - If you are in a position to delegate, do it. Always put a tickler alert in your calendar to remind you to check on the progress of those you have charged with duties.

The goal here is to free your mind and enable it to focus on one project at a time. All other projects and issues not related to the current project should be filed away in a place where they can be found easily. Tickler alerts remind you to review them on a regular basis. Until that time, focus on the task at hand.

Focus is incredibly powerful but can also be dangerous. Remember the sunlight example. You don't want to light a fire at work and melt down your family at the same time. Focus but stay balanced. We'll talk more about balance later.

The Quadrant Model for Focus

The quadrant model is a priority tool in many disciplines, often used in time management. I find it more helpful in the realm of focus.

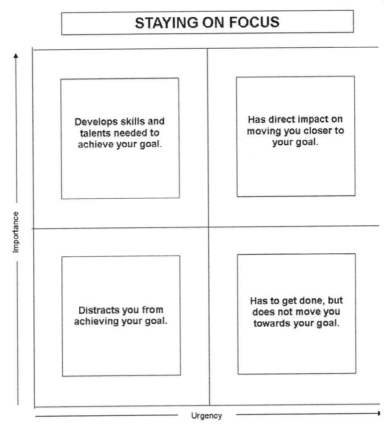

STAYING ON FOCUS

Develops skills and talents needed to achieve your goal.

Has direct impact on moving you closer to your goal.

Distracts you from achieving your goal.

Has to get done, but does not move you towards your goal.

Importance

Urgency

Printable worksheets can be downloaded from
WhereDoIGoFromHere.net

When planning daily, weekly, and monthly activities, ask yourself, "Where does this activity fit in the Focus Quadrant?" For many of us, about 70% of our lives fit into the "urgent, but not directly moving us toward our goal" category. We have to work at our day job, buy the groceries, feed the family, go to our kids' ball games and school plays, and take care of the mundane but urgent needs like paying the taxes, visiting relatives, etc. The difference between those who fulfill their goals and aspirations and those who do not is what they do with the remaining 30% of their time.

If you have planned your action steps correctly, you can consistently move toward your goal without disrupting other important aspects of your life. Those who spend just an hour a day taking steps toward their goal will achieve and experience success in life. Those who live with excuses like, "I'm too tired," or "The goal is too hard," or "This is taking too long," will go nowhere. Those who seek to force their goal without taking care of the critical needs of job and family may achieve their goal, but their lives often turn into train wrecks.

Create a Balance Wheel

I believe that being successful means having a balance of success stories across the many areas of your life. You can't truly be considered successful in your business life if your home life is in shambles.
- Zig Ziglar

This little device is a favorite among business and personal coaches. It allows you to see where you are in balance and where you need to apply more attention.

Draw a circle that takes up most of the space on a blank sheet of paper. Next, draw four lines that intersect in the center. You now have something that resembles a sliced pie with eight pieces. Label each line on the outside of the circle.

Business Success
Financial Security
Stress Free Life
Family
Personal Fulfillment
Spiritual Life
Recreation
Health

Imagine each line having ten tick marks on it. Zero is in the center, and ten is on the circumference. Place a dot on a number on each line indicating how you feel you're doing in each area. Rate your satisfaction in each area from 0 to 10, with 0 being highly dissatisfied and 10 being very satisfied. Connect the dots. Now you have a picture of how balanced your life is. If this were a wheel on your vehicle, how smooth a ride would you have? The wheel is your visual guide to areas you may need to focus on for a while.

Balance Wheel Exercise

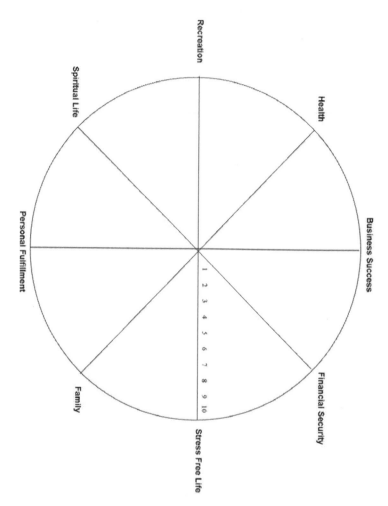

Printable worksheets can be downloaded from
WhereDoIGoFromHere.net

Getting Out of Balance on Purpose

Some goals are more demanding than others. Life situations may present opportunities that should not be ignored. You may have to get out of balance from time to time. Say, for example, you're starting a new business venture, or your company is introducing a new product. These are moments of opportunity. If the time is right, you may want to move to an out of balance position for 30 to 60 days. Don't do this if there is a new baby in the house or there are other high priority matters that demand your attention. If that's the case, relax, other opportunities will always come. But if the time is right, get your family's agreement to be out of balance for 60 days. Cut back on all other commitments and focus on a single venture. You will be amazed at how much you can accomplish. At the end of the 60 days, get back in balance. Return to your balance wheel and reassess you life. Devote more attention to your family, friends, and civic responsibilities again. You will find that the momentum created in that brief period of focus will reap benefits far into the future.

Excuse-Free Living

Ninety-nine percent of the failures come from people who have the habit of making excuses.
- George Washington Carver

The number one cause for personal or business failure is accepting your own excuses.

> I'm too busy.
> I'm too tired.
> I have too many kids.
> I'm too broke.

I don't know the right people.
I never seem to get ahead.

If you have accepted these or similar excuses about
yourself, you have probably never accomplished as much
with your life as possible. Remember King Solomon and
the *Book of Proverbs* in the *Bible* puts it this way.

> Tell me, lazy, how long are you just going to lie
> around?
> When are you going to get up and do something?
> Sleep in whenever you like.
> Enjoy your naps.
> Sit back and rest awhile.
> Then, poverty will rob you like a thief.[31]

The first thing that happens when you live by your own
excuses is that you accept the excuses of people around
you.

Jim was a car salesman. He did okay, if you define *okay* as
meeting the minimum sales quota each month. He never
really tried to do better. He didn't think he could. He didn't
think he deserved it. He lived from one excuse to another.
He had an excuse for coming in late. He had an excuse for
his multiple divorces. He had an excuse for every customer
who did not buy a car. Of course, every customer who did
not buy a car had an excuse. Jim just made their excuse his
excuse. When Jim learned that it was okay to make a
mistake, but not okay to make an excuse, his life changed.
He accepted responsibility. If he came to work late, there
was no excuse. He had made a mistake. Mistakes were
preventable. Excuses were not. So he stopped arriving at
work late. He invested time learning his products so he
could stop telling his customers that he didn't know what
options were available on certain models. No more excuses.

He also stopped accepting excuses from his customers. If they said, "I'm not ready to buy today," he would ask, "Why not?" Then he would refuse to accept their excuse. "If you can't buy a car, then why are you shopping? If you can buy a car, then why waste time? If you find what you want and the deal makes sense, just do it." If they said, "I can't afford $20,000 for a new car," he would ask, "What can you afford? Let's find something in your price range." Within weeks, he was top salesman in the dealership.

Personal coaching is an entire industry that's based on the simple principle of accountability. Decide what you're going to do. Tell your coach what you're going to do. Be accountable to get it done. No more excuses.

Prioritize Your Goals

The key is not to prioritize what's on your schedule, but to schedule your priorities.
- Stephen Covey

Prioritization is one of the most difficult things we do in life. And, because it's one of our most critical tasks, we need to do it every day.

How many goals are on your goal board? Ten? Fifty? One hundred?

How can you accomplish all those goals? One goal at a time.

The natural tendency is to want to accomplish everything at once. All of our goals seem so important to us. However, if we try to do them all at the same time, we will accomplish nothing.

What goal is most important to you? What goal is the easiest to accomplish? What goal do you need to tackle immediately? What goal, if accomplished, would make everything else in your life better or easier?

In Chapter 2, when we first started setting goals, I said that it's important to focus on only one to three goals at a time. I made the point that it was critical that your goals were supported by your core values. Still, it is quite likely that you had difficulty selecting only three goals to focus on. Also, as time goes on, life changes. New challenges require an adjustment of goal priorities. If you don't prioritize carefully, immediate and critical issues will rob you of your ability to focus on the long-term ultimate goals that lead you to the fulfillment of your life vision.

The reality is that your priorities change almost daily. Priorities can become fuzzy. In such times, it is important to take a moment to prioritize your goals. There are four factors to take into account when prioritizing your goals.

- Immediacy
- Simplicity
- Importance
- Impact

Immediate goals rise to the top of the list. If it is April 14 and your taxes are not filed, you know what goal is number one that day.

You may want to finish some simple, easy-to-accomplish goals. It can be a great source of encouragement to know you have accomplished some of your goals. Also, getting those simple goals out of the way frees your mental space for other more important goals.

Important goals move you toward your ultimate life vision. These could be getting a degree or certification, making important associate connections, or finishing a project that will earn you valuable recognition.

Major-impact goals are those that can change everything in your life. I like to call them "winning touchdown" goals. For someone in an academic field, a major-impact goal might be getting a doctorate from a prestigious university. For an entertainer, it might be a coveted television appearance. For me, a "winning touchdown" goal was the book you hold in your hands.

The following worksheet will help you prioritize your goals when life seems to get out-of-hand. List all your goals in the left-hand column. Assign a numerical value of one through five for each aspect of simplicity, importance, and impact, with one being the least simple, important, or impactful and five being the most. Tally up the numbers in the right-hand column for each goal. This will give you a visual reference that can help you choose which goals to focus on. One goal may become the obvious priority. Several goals may be near equal in priority. Try to get back to one to three goals to focus on, even if only for today. Remember *Stillness*. Take a few deep breaths. Quiet your mental chatter. Listen to your intuition. Choose your priorities.

Change the world one goal at a time.

Goal Prioritization Worksheet

Assign a value of 1-5 for each aspect of your goals. Total the values to help you prioritize your goals.

					Goal	Simplicity	Importance	Impact	Total

Slay Over-Commitment

Why is it so many of us have such a hard time saying no? Our kids want us to take them to the movies. The PTA asks us to coordinate the next fund-raiser. Our spouse wants us to go away for a weekend. Our church invites us to teach a class. Our boss wants us to stay a few extra hours to go over the latest report or prepare the next presentation. Then, when friends invite us to dinner, we look at our calendar and say, "I have an opening for three hours four weeks from this Thursday night. Does that work for you?" Sometimes we even feel organized or in control, because we have everything so neatly written in block letters in our planner. The truth is that we are completely out of control. Everyone else is in control of our lives. We're just along for the ride.

You have expended a good deal of time and effort to identify and prioritize your goals. I repeat, <u>YOUR</u> goals. Keep your goals always in your mind. If you feel tempted to forsake your goals for someone else's, go back to Chapter 4. Identify the emotional wound or need that is causing you to choose the self-destructive path of pleasing someone else instead of fulfilling your own destiny. I'm not saying you should become a recluse, ignore the needs of others, or become just plain mean, being so fervently in pursuit of what you want that you cut down anyone who is in your way. What I do recommend is that you treat yourself with respect and continue on your chosen path to fulfill your values and accomplish your goals. In the end, everyone around you will be glad to know the fulfilled and peaceful you.

Believe it or not, you can say no and still be a good person. You will discover that you can accomplish a lot more for yourself, for your family, and for the world around you when you're in control of your life. Don't let yourself be controlled by anyone willing to yank on your heartstrings.

Guided Meditation:
Your Place of Inspiration

A CD of this meditation is available from Amazon.com and other retail outlets.

Find a place where you will not be observed or disturbed.

Sit up straight in a comfortable position.

Close your eyes.

Allow yourself to breathe naturally. Take breath in. Let breath out.

Now take a deep cleansing breath in through your nose, if possible. Notice the rise and fall of your chest and abdomen. Notice the sense of chill as the cool air passes through your nostrils. Blow it all out, pushing up with your diaphragm to empty your lungs completely. Take a second cleansing breath to rejuvenate your lungs with fresh air.

Take a few upper breaths, focusing on pushing the air into the chest portion of your lungs. Take your fingertips and touch your heart. Feel your chest move up and down as you take each breath. Breathe in, through your nose if possible, and out through your mouth. If you can't breathe that way, don't worry. That technique is just a way to help take your mind off other things and concentrate on your breath.

Now take a few lower breaths, focusing on pushing air as deeply into your abdomen as possible. Again, breathe in, through your nose if possible, and out through your mouth. As you inhale, imagine yourself breathing in positive

energy. As you exhale, imagine yourself breathing out negative energy. Say to yourself:

> *Breathe in peace; breathe out anxiety.*
> *Breathe in faith; breathe out doubt.*
> *Breathe in love; breathe out indifference.*
> *Breathe in hope; breathe out despair.*
> *Breathe in confidence; breathe out timidity.*

Release thoughts or feelings of stress or anxiety. Thoughts about problems at work or home may rush in at this point. That's normal. Don't fight the thoughts. Just acknowledge them and let them slip away.

Relax your body. Focus on your head. Recognize any tension in your scalp, face, or jaw. Will each area to relax. Let your jaw slip down slightly into a relaxed position. Now focus on your neck and shoulders. Again, recognize any tension and will each area to relax. Repeat this relaxation technique for your arms and chest. As you focus on your diaphragm, your breathing may alter a bit. You may begin to breathe a little more deeply and regularly as if asleep. Continue the technique, moving down your body until you reach your toes. Take a moment to realize that you are fully relaxed.

As before, focus on your breath. Empty yourself of other thoughts. Notice your sense of peace. Notice your awareness of sounds around you. Are there other feelings or sensations? Do you find yourself stretching or yawning? Are there other manifestations of tension release? Whatever your body wants to do in this state is okay. Just let yourself relax.

Now take a deep breath and let it all out. Again.

Take a deep breath. Imagine filling your body with air. Now release. Allow the air to leave your body and with it, all tension and anxiety.

Take another deep breath. Now release. Allow the air to leave your body, and with it, all fear about your future.

As you continue to take deep breaths, focus on the air rushing into your lungs. Breath is energy. Breath is life.

Picture the breath energy flowing into your brain, energizing your thoughts.

Continue focusing on your breath.

Your mind is illuminated by the energy of your breath.

Continue to focus on your breath.

As new thoughts and visions come to light in the illumination of your breath, you feel a greater sense of peace.

Continue to focus on your breath.

In the recesses of your creative imagination, you discover a hope and confidence you didn't know you had.

Continue to focus on your breath.

The knowledge of the pathway to success is there. You know it. You can sense it. Hope and confidence are giving birth to excitement and exhilaration at the thought of your journey ahead.

Continue to focus on your breath.

Take a deep breath. Feel the energy. Let it all out. Open your eyes.

Now take a notepad and jot down some notes of what you discovered.

Notes from Your Guided Meditation

_____

_____

_____

_____

_____

_____

_____

_____

_____

_____

_____

_____

CHAPTER 10

The Journey Never Ends

Arriving at one goal is the starting point to another.
- John Dewey

In a society of instant food and instant entertainment, we often think we should experience instant proficiency or instant success. Well, life doesn't usually work that way. It takes time, effort, practice, and patience to get proficient at a skill and enjoy success from it.

No matter how good you are at what you do, there is always room for improvement. Improvement is not a luxury. When you stop improving, you start deteriorating. The path of deterioration leads to destruction, often in the form of loss of a job, loss of a career, loss of a relationship, even loss of life itself. How do you excel at what you do? Very simple - keep getting better.

So how do you keep improving? Follow the steps in this book. Just keep reviewing and applying the principles. Reassess your values. Set new goals. Imagine a clearer vision. Create new affirmations. Improve your processes. Attain new heights.

If you make it your constant, continual, determined habit to improve on a daily basis, you will soon excel in your chosen field.

Daily ask yourself, "What is one small step I can make today to improve my skill at _____?" Write it down in your planner. Review it throughout the day until it's accomplished.

It doesn't matter if the step is small as long as your application is consistent. Many small steps will make a long and fruitful journey.

Practice doesn't necessarily make for perfection, but it does get you one step closer.

In fact, the old adage that practice makes perfect isn't entirely true. Perfection is a foolish goal. It is unattainable. It is helpful to restate the proverb, "Practice makes progress." To seek to be a little closer to perfection each day is an excellent goal.

Whatever you do, make sure you learn it correctly the first time. Retraining is more difficult than learning it right the first time. Early in your career, you should seek out a mentor, hire a personal coach, and do whatever it takes to set the proper habits from the beginning. Your efforts will pay great dividends down the road.

A Life Lesson from the Game of Chess

In chess, each player begins with the same sixteen pieces on the same 64 square board. Both players begin even, and what sits before them is all they have to work with. There are no magic wands and no wizards to stir the pieces about. Each player is responsible for their moves and must respond to their opponent's move. As the game progresses, the game board changes. Some pieces are taken off the board as they are captured by an opponent. In a sense, with each move, the game begins anew, but with the pieces in different positions. At each turn, the player must deal with the reality of the new formation. It's a foolish waste of energy to wish you had an extra queen or that your knight was on a different square.

The only place to begin is where you are right now. All you have to work with is reality.

Too often, we waste time and mental energy wishing we were in a different position than we are. We wish we had received more breaks. We wish we had a different degree. We wish we had made different choices.

The bad news is that we cannot change the past that brought us to where we are today. The good news is that the next move is ours to take. The next break is ours to make.

If life were a game of chess, what would be your next move?

Do Something

Do you want to know who you are? Don't ask. Act! Action will delineate and define you.
- Thomas Jefferson

One key to constant improvement is staying motivated. The best way to stay motivated is to do something. Do anything. It's best if what you do moves you toward the goal you're trying to achieve, but even if not, just do it.

If you're unmotivated to keeping your desk clean, just read and file the letter that's staring you in the face. Pay the bill in the in-box. If you can't afford to pay it, put it in a file labeled "Bills To Pay." After a few simple steps, you may find that you are encouraged by your progress and you decide to keep going. If not, go outside and take a walk.

Clear your head and get your blood flowing. Then, come back and do something.

Remember Newton's law of motion. Any object in motion tends to stay in motion. Any object at rest tends to stay at rest. Don't be trapped by inactivity. Keep moving.

The Three Faiths

Try not to become a man of success, but rather try to become a man of value....Only a life lived for others is a life worthwhile.
- Albert Einstein

Throughout your life, your success will depend on how you cultivate the three faiths.

  - Faith in God: However you define the concept.
  - Faith in yourself: Your talents, abilities, wisdom, and dedication.
  - Faith in those who surround and support you: Especially your spouse, family, friends, coworkers, and business associates.

Everyday do something to cultivate each of the three faiths.

Spend quiet time developing your spirituality. Pray, meditate, and do spiritual reading in your own tradition. Learn about other traditions for the purpose of understanding, tolerance, and compassion.

Everyday do something for self-improvement. Read a book. Learn a new language. Practice a skill. Become a better person.

Everyday do something that improves your relationship with the people who live and work around you. Help your spouse. Hug your kids. Assist a coworker. Call a business associate just to see how they're doing.
Simple steps will make your life richer and more enjoyable.

And, in everything, be thankful.

Nothing Changes Your Attitude Like Gratitude

Gratitude unlocks the fullness of life. It turns what we have into enough, and more. It turns denial into acceptance, chaos to order, confusion to clarity. It can turn a meal into a feast, a house into a home, a stranger into a friend.
- Melody Beattie

A farmer's favorite stallion ran away. Rather than giving into anger, the farmer simply prayed, "Thank you God for my horse. May he find peace wherever he roams." A few days later, his stallion returned with two wild mares. The farmer prayed, "Thank you God for the new mares. May they find peace in my stable." The farmer's son was breaking the mares when he was thrown and broke his leg. The farmer prayed, "Thank you God for my son. May he find peace in his suffering." A few days later, the local warlord rode into the village pressing young able-bodied men into military service. The farmer prayed, "Thank you God for protecting my son. May our days be filled with your peace."

The moral to the story is simple. Good and bad are not always evident in the present. Gratitude expresses a trust that God can and will bring about a better future. It often triggers a release of grace into our lives.

A failed relationship can pave the way to a more fulfilling one. A failed business can teach lessons that make the next business venture unbelievably profitable.
Whatever happens, find your place of gratitude and watch miracles unfold.

Keep Score

Do you remember when you were growing up? The operative word here is 'growing'. For many of us, our parents measured our growth by marking a line on the wall each year on our birthday. I, for one, really looked forward to seeing my new mark each year. I always felt big and proud when the marks continued to climb the wall. I was keeping score of my growth.

At some point, we stop getting taller, but we should never stop growing. And we should never stop measuring our growth. We just grow in different ways and use different measurements. The runner keeps track of times. The batter tracks base hits.

What business are you in? What can your measurements be? In business, these are called metrics, but it's really just score keeping. The more comprehensive the score keeping, the better the overall picture and the more motivating it can become.

A salesperson might track:
- Phone calls
- Appointments
- Sales
- Follow-up
- Referrals
- Repeat sales

You notice I didn't just stop at the sale, but went on to measure follow-up, referrals, and repeat sales. The fact that these activities will be tracked and measured motivates the salesperson to do good follow-up, ask for the referral, and maintain a relationship with the client in order to get repeat sales. Assign a point value for the activities.

- Phone calls = 1 point
- Appointments = 10 points
- Sales = 20 points
- Follow up = 10 points
- Referrals = 20 points
- Repeat sales = 30 points

This system is designed to encourage building relationships that result in repeat sales. Your own business will likely have different activities and different point values. Think of what you want to accomplish, and design your own system to reward the activity that brings you the greatest benefit.

Keep track of your daily/weekly/monthly points. Make a graph and post it where you can see it. You will be surprised at how motivating this can be. When you see yourself slipping behind, you will want to do more activity to get your graph up. As your graph climbs, so will your sales.

The principle applies far beyond the sales profession. A banker might measure total deposits, new depositors, new loans, total receivables, etc. Military personnel can measure citations received and rank advancement. Students have built in scores with grade point averages and degrees received. Teachers and scientists measure professional publications. Consultants, attorneys, or CPAs may measure total clients or billable hours. If you're a corporate employee, read over your job description carefully to determine metrics you can target to assist your movement up the corporate ladder. Even a stay-at-home parent can measure keeping the monthly food bill under budget, reduction of children's sick days, or home projects completed. There are many measurements to use.

Score keeping is always motivational. Either it encourages because you see objective proof that you're improving, or it reveals areas that need special attention.

Focus on the 20% that Makes You 80%

An Italian economist, Vilfredo Pareto, noticed that 80% of the land was in possession of 20% of the population. He committed himself to studying the phenomenon and discovered that the same ratio applied to a wide variety of circumstances.[32]

For example, say you own a coffee shop conveniently located between a university and a business district. A quick look around reveals that the majority of your customers are students, latté and laptop in hand. But an analysis of your sales reveals that the majority of your revenues come from business people hosting lunches and small meetings in your shop. While there are more students in your shop at any given time, the per capita spending of the professionals who frequent the shop is three times the per capita spending of the students. Armed with that knowledge, you can now create ways to attract more business professionals to your shop. Perhaps you can set a portion of your shop aside to be reserved for business lunches and presentations. Market the space as the Imagination Room. "Think out of the box. Get away from the office. Hold your meetings in our Imagination Room. Find fresh ideas in new places."

Sales people who track closure rate by lead source can focus on lead sources that produce the best results. Network marketers who focus on down-lines that are growing the fastest will be more successful than those who focus on trying to get lackluster performers to change.

A key to success is to discover who or what the 20% is and focus on it.

Overcome Obstacles

If you're trying to achieve, there will be roadblocks. I've had them; everybody has had them. But obstacles don't have to stop you. If you run into a wall, don't turn around and give up. Figure out how to climb it, go through it, or work around it.
- Michael Jordan

Every individual's path to success includes overcoming setbacks. If you do not have an affirmation about resilience, you might consider creating one now.

I read about a politician who lost far more elections than he won, but he never quit trying. He went on to become President of the United States and is considered by many to be one of the finest presidents in our history. His image is carved into Mount Rushmore. His name was Abraham Lincoln.

On your path to fulfilling the goals you set down in this book, you will experience failure. Your ultimate success will have more to do with how you handle those failures than how smart or talented you are.

Here are two activities to help develop your quality of resilience.

1. Develop your imagination.

One reason children are so resilient is that they have well-developed imaginations. If they want to play pirate but don't have a toy sword, they use a stick. As soon as they hear the word no, their mental wheels start turning to find a different way of asking.

Your imagination can provide you with alternatives so that when one method fails, you can try another.

Practicing *Stillness* each day will naturally develop your imagination. Here are a few other ideas to help develop imagination.
- Instead of watching a movie, read a book.
- Instead of reading a book, write a short story.
- Watch clouds and imagine what they are (a favorite among children).
- Read your vision every day with profound emotion. Place yourself in your vision. Play a little movie in your head of you living your dream.

2. Play games.

Games teach us to react to the unexpected. It doesn't matter if it's playing checkers with an old friend or pick-up basketball with strangers at the gym. Games develop flexibility, confidence, and a positive attitude.

Overcoming Obstacles Exercise

Write down an obstacle that holds you back from fulfilling your goal. (For example, it can be lack of time, insufficient capital, not knowing the right people, etc.)

_____

Write down at least five creative ways of overcoming that obstacle.

1. _____

2. _____

3. _____

4. _____

5. _____

From the preceding list, choose one you will do to overcome that obstacle and achieve your goal.

_____

Make a commitment.

Today I will:

_____

This week I will:

_____

On an ongoing basis, I will:

_____

Stillness as a Gateway to your Intuition

The creative is the place where no one else has ever been. You have to leave the city of your comfort and go into the wilderness of your intuition. What you'll discover will be wonderful. What you'll discover is yourself.
- Alan Alda

Prayer, meditation, yoga, mindfulness, and even self-hypnosis all share common technical elements with the practice of *Stillness*. Each employs the three elements of intentional breathing, relaxation, and focus. Each brings the practitioner into a quiet, peaceful mental state. The subtle differences lie in the heart and intention of the practitioner.

A key purpose of *Stillness*, as I have taught it here, is to quiet your mind in order to think more clearly. It also gets you in touch with the forgotten thoughts and memories that lie beneath the surface chatter of your conscious mind. Everything you have ever read, heard, or experienced is locked away somewhere in your brain. These memories bubble to the surface in the form of intuition that can give you insight. These insights can provide direction and help you avoid mistakes.

How fast is the speed of thought? Literally billions of thoughts race through your mind every second. Calculations at the University of Alberta demonstrate that the human brain performs 20 million billion calculations per second.[33] Most are subconscious.

I discussed *Stillness* in the first chapter and have referred to it throughout the book. I am coming back to it now because of the importance for the practice of *Stillness* to become a daily practice. Your mind is constantly exploring new avenues. Imagining new solutions. Trailblazing new paths. However, it is far too easy to become so embroiled in the many day-to-day demands and never stop to listen to the quiet whisperings of your inner genius.

It is important to your long-term success and general wellbeing to get in touch with your creative imagination on a daily basis. Only when your conscious mind is quiet and still can you bring the genius of your intuitive mind to the surface.

Make it your daily habit to practice *Stillness* and listen to the wisdom of your inner genius.

Guided Meditation:
Your Personal Place of Peace

A CD of this meditation is available from Amazon.com and other retail outlets.

Find a place where you will not be observed or disturbed.

Sit up straight in a comfortable position.

Close your eyes.

Allow yourself to breathe naturally. Take breath in. Let breath out.

Now take a deep cleansing breath in through your nose, if possible. Notice the rise and fall of your chest and abdomen. Notice the sense of chill as the cool air passes through your nostrils. Blow it all out, pushing up with your diaphragm to empty your lungs completely. Take a second cleansing breath to rejuvenate your lungs with fresh air.

Take a few upper breaths, focusing on pushing the air into the chest portion of your lungs. Take your fingertips and touch your heart. Feel your chest move up and down as you take each breath. Breathe in, through your nose if possible, and out through your mouth. If you can't breathe that way, don't worry. That technique is just a way to help take your mind off other things and concentrate on your breath.

Now take a few lower breaths, focusing on pushing air as deeply into your abdomen as possible. Again, breathe in, through your nose if possible, and out through your mouth. As you inhale, imagine yourself breathing in positive

energy. As you exhale, imagine yourself breathing out
negative energy. Say to yourself:

Breathe in peace; breathe out anxiety.
Breathe in faith; breathe out doubt.
Breathe in love; breathe out indifference.
Breathe in hope; breathe out despair.
Breathe in confidence; breathe out timidity.

Let thoughts and feelings of stress or anxiety melt away
from your mind. Thoughts about problems at work or home
may rush in at this point. That's normal. Don't fight the
thoughts. Just acknowledge them and let them slip away.

Relax your body. Focus on your head. Recognize any
tension in your scalp, face, or jaw. Will each area to relax.
Let your jaw slip down slightly into a relaxed position.
Now focus on your neck and shoulders. Again, recognize
any tension and will each area to relax. Repeat this
relaxation technique for your arms and chest. As you focus
on your diaphragm, your breathing may alter a bit. You
may begin to breathe a little more deeply and regularly as if
asleep. Continue the technique, moving down your body
until you reach your toes. Take a moment to realize that
you are fully relaxed.

As before, focus on your breath. Empty yourself of other
thoughts. Notice your sense of peace. Notice your
awareness of sounds around you. Are there other feelings
or sensations? Do you find yourself stretching or yawning?
Are there other manifestations of tension release? Whatever
your body wants to do in this state is okay. Just let yourself
relax.

Now take a deep breath and let it all out. Again.

Take a deep breath. Imagine filling your body with air. Now release. Allow the air to leave your body and with it, all tension and anxiety.

Take another deep breath. Now release. Allow the air to leave your body, and with it, all fear about your future.

As you continue to take deep breaths, focus on the air rushing into your lungs. Breath is energy. Breath is life.

Picture the breath energy flowing into your brain, energizing your thoughts.

Continue focusing on your breath.

Your mind is illuminated by the energy of your breath.

Continue to focus on your breath.

Allow your creative imagination to create in your mind your peaceful place. You may find yourself sitting on a mountaintop looking over the vast expanse of the world. You may find yourself sitting beside a stream, or on a beach looking into the raw power of a great ocean. Or, you may envision yourself sitting in a comfortable room with loved ones around you. Perhaps you're sitting at a desk in an office feeling a great sense of accomplishment. There is no right or wrong place. Your peaceful place is yours alone. It is the fulfillment of your passion. Rest there for a while.

Continue to focus on your breath.

Notice the sights of your peaceful place. Hear the sounds. Imagine the smells. You have followed your personal journey, your quest to success. Rest.

Continue to focus on your breath.

You feel yourself being rejuvenated. You're growing stronger. You're discovering new confidence. Rest.

Continue to focus on your breath.

It is okay for your mind to be empty at this point.

It is okay to let your mind wander on its own tangents.

You may sense a new thought or inspiration.

Or, you may just relax in quietness and *Stillness*.

Take a deep breath. Feel the energy. Let it all out. Open your eyes.

Now take a notepad and jot down your discoveries.

Notes from Your Guided Meditation

_____

_____

_____

_____

_____

_____

_____

_____

_____

_____

_____

_____

_____

Printable worksheets can be downloaded from
WhereDoIGoFromHere.net

CHAPTER 11

A Backpack for the Journey

Go confidently in the direction of your dreams. Live the life you have imagined.
- Henry David Thoreau

At this point, you have:
- Identified your core values.
- Developed an ultimate vision for your life.
- Created goals that will propel you to your life's vision.
- Drawn up a plan of action steps that will move you along your path.
- Determined milestones and rewards to keep you motivated.

Now it's time to think about a backpack of goodies to take along with you on your journey. After all, you might get hungry along the way. We're not talking about cheese and crackers here, but food for your soul on lonely nights along the road.

Permission Slip

The first thing I am putting in your road pack is a permission slip. This permission slip gives you permission to:
- Ignore everyone who knows what is good for you. Goal setting is supposed to be fun and motivating. However, if other people are setting your goals for you, it becomes depressing and debilitating. It's your life and your goals. Choose what you want.

- Devote some time each day to having fun. Enjoy life. You will find that a little joy goes a long way in energizing you to fulfill your life's purpose and vision.
- Take as long as you need to complete your goals and fulfill your life's vision. Timetables never seem to work out the way we expect. Be patient.
- Make a mistake every now and then. Fear of making mistakes keeps people from trying. That's the worst mistake of all. Mistakes will happen. Don't let them stop you.
- Change your mind and direction if you want to. The road to your future is not a straight path. You will make new discoveries along the way that will affect what you want out of life. There have been many times I have gone back through the entire process to determine if I am still on the track I desire. If not, I make adjustments and set off in a new direction. Be flexible.

Purpose

It's important to carry a life-purpose in your backpack. Have you ever wondered if there is a purpose to the struggles, the joys, the accomplishments, the failures, and even the sufferings of life? Being able to see a purpose in your life is critical to having an unshakeable sense of value and self-worth beyond such externals as wealth and prestige.

Being cynical is a popular attitude in today's world. Modern people tend to disregard things that are metaphysical or eternal and focus on a day-to-day drudgery where they simply survive until they die. Studies consistently demonstrate that people who have a sense of purpose in life are happier and more successful than those who consider such concepts as mythical, superstitious, or just plain nonsense. Many people allow their reliance on technology to erase their reliance on God. They dare not believe in God or hope that he is somehow giving them purpose and help on life's journey. If we ignore that there is something greater than ourselves, it is ourselves that we are selling short. If we do not believe in an ultimate good in the universe, then it is difficult to find inspiration to make ourselves better. If there is no Master in the cosmos, then there can be no purpose for us or anything else in it.

The intention of this book is not to make you into a religious person, but to help you find your highest self and best success. Again, I encourage you to engage in the daily practice of *Stillness*. Your life-purpose is not something you can search for and find. However, if you spend time each day silencing the incessant chatter of your fears and concerns, your life-purpose will come to you when you're ready for it, because it's always been in you.

Partners

Coming together is a beginning; keeping together is progress; working together is success.
- Henry Ford

You don't need to make this journey alone. Since Adam and Eve, the hardships of life have been made easier with a partner.

If you're married, I hope your spouse is your best partner and biggest fan. I realize that not everyone is married and not all spouses are supportive. Even if you are fortunate enough to have a supportive spouse, their interests and talents may not lend themselves to directly support your endeavors. It is important for spouses to have a unified life vision. However, they may take different paths to that vision.

Business partners, mastermind groups, best friends, co-workers, and business associates can all contribute to a sense of partnership in life. Develop an inner circle of close friends and associates whom you can trust and speak with freely. They may not have answers, but just processing aloud can be extremely helpful.

Everyone is familiar with Steve Jobs of Apple Computer. However, it was the other Steve of Apple who invented the Apple I and Apple II computers. Steve Wozniak was Steve Jobs' business partner at Apple and the technical genius that transformed Steve Jobs' vision into hardware.

Other partners can include consultants, business or life coaches, ministers or religious leaders, authors, mentors, and motivational speakers. Tap into the knowledge and experience of those around you or those who have shared their knowledge in books or online.

Don't let yourself be alone on your journey. Take time to share with and listen to others.

Shared pain always decreases. Shared joy always increases. Shared wisdom always grows.

Humor

You will need to take a sense of humor with you in your backpack if you hope to succeed in life. Laughter relieves tension and makes life generally more bearable. None of us has everything so figured out that we don't have plenty of opportunities to laugh at ourselves.

We all intuitively know that laughter makes us feel better. New scientific studies have documented many of the benefits of laughter. Laughter helps you de-stress and relax.

It fosters the release of endorphins and boosts your immune system. It even increases blood flow and may help prevent certain heart diseases.[34]

Find time for some laughter each day. Watch a funny TV program. Read a few of those joke emails that are stacking up in your inbox. I have a friend who is an avid reader of comics in the local newspaper. When one strikes him particularly funny, he cuts it out and puts it in a box he keeps in his closet. If he is feeling downtrodden or upset, he pulls down the box and begins reading. In a few minutes, he finds himself renewed with energy and a fresh perspective on life.

Joy

Finally, don't forget to place several helpings of joy into your pack. Joy will give you strength on your journey that may often be difficult.

Here are a few steps you can take to find joy when the night is dark.
- **Get some perspective**. You are not alone in your trial. Many have faced it before you and overcome. Their stories are passed down to encourage us. Some have failed and have slipped out of memory. Choose.
- **Find purpose**. You have a purpose in life. There is a purpose in this current trial. Find it. Hold onto it.
- **Help someone in need**. There is always someone worse off than you are. You have something to give. Sometimes a cheerful smile, a word of encouragement, and the feel of a human touch can make the difference between life and death for someone. Give of yourself.
- **Learn something new**. Expanding your breadth of knowledge is one of life's greatest joys. Read a good

book, take a class, talk to your coach or mentor. Keep learning.

Your life's journey should be pleasurable in every way. Enjoy it.

Endnotes

1   Harry Bradford, *America Deal in the Bathtub.* (*The Huffington Post* August, 2011).

2   "Why does Apolo Anton Ohno yawn before his races?" *China Daily* (February, 2010).

3   Peter Delevett, "Naval Ravikant of Angel List went from dot-com pariah to Silicon Valley power broker," *San Jose Mercury News* (February, 2013).

4   "David Filo & Jerry Yang," *Entrepreneur.com* (October 9, 2008).

5   Gail Mathews, *Study Backs up Strategies for Achieving Goals,* (Dominican University of California: dominican.edu).

6   Laura Denktash, *Use Visualization Techniques When Writing To Stay On Track.* (LauraDekntash.com May 3, 2011).

7   Eric Velazquez, "How Ali Became the Greatest" *Muscle and Performance Magazine* (2012).

8   Jim Flick and Jack Nicklaus, "Go to the Movies," *Golf Digest* (June 2010).

9   Lynne McTaggart, *The Intention Experiment: Using Your Thoughts to Change Your Life and the World.* (2007).

10   Colossians 1:12 (translated by the author).

11   "Entrepreneur's Hall of Fame: Phineas Taylor (P.T.) Barnum," *Let's Talk Business Network, Inc* (2007).

12   Peter Cowie, *Coppola* (Da Capo Press, 1994).

13   Neal Gabler, *Walt Disney: The Triumph of the American Imagination.* (Random House 2006).

14   Clare O'Connor, "Fourth Time's A Charm: How Donald Trump Made Bankruptcy Work For Him," *Forbes.com* (April 29, 2011).

15   Proverbs 24:16 (translated by the author).

16   Rudyard Kipling, *The White Man's Burden* (1899).

17   Based on a quote from *The Seven Pillars of Wisdom* by T. E. Lawrence. "All men dream, but not equally. Those

who dream by night in the dusty recesses of their minds, wake in the day to find that it was vanity: but the dreamers of the day are dangerous men, for they may act on their dreams with open eyes, to make them possible."

18   Heather Barry Kappes and Gabriele Oettingen, "Positive Fantasies About Idealized Futures Sap Energy," *Journal of Experimental Social Psychology* (February, 2011).

19   Luke 18:1-7 (translated by the author).

20   Matthew 13:31,32 (translated by the author).

21   Luke 6:38 (translated by the author).

22   Jane Porter, "Entrepreneurs who Turned Hobbies Into Million-Dollar Businesses," *Entrepreneur.com* (September, 2012).

23   Jeff Wallenfeldt, "Luciano Benetton"*Britannica.com* (2013).

24   Norman Vincent Peale, *The Power of Positive Thinking.*

25   Hippoocrates *The Nature of Man.* (circa 400 BC).

26   Jamie McManus, MD., *How Well do you Understand the Shaklee Difference?*

27   Sonja Lyubomirsky, *The How of Happiness.* (The Penguin Press 2008).

28   Daniel Goleman, "A Feel-Good Theory: A Smile Affects Mood." *The New York Times* (July 18, 1989).

29   Matthew J Hertenstein, Carrie A. Hansel, Alissa M. Butts, and Sarah N. Hile. *Smile intensity in photographs predicts divorce later in life.* (Springer Science+Business Media, LLC. 2009).

30   Chesley B Sullenberge and Jeffrey Zaslow, *Highest Duty: My Search for What Really Matters* (2009).

31   Proverbs 6:9-11 (translated by the author).

32   Vilfredo Pareto: *Manuale di Economia Politica* (1909).

33   Chris Westbury, *How Fast does the Human Brain Compute* (University of Alberta ualberta.ca).

[34]   Michelle Murray, *Laughter is the Best Medicine for Your Heart* University of Maryland Medical Center (2009).

NOTES

238

NOTES

NOTES

Made in the USA
Middletown, DE
13 March 2019